Effective Government Accounting

Also by A. Premchand

Control of Public Expenditure in India (1966)

Performance Budgeting (1969)

*Government Budgeting and Expenditure Controls (1983)

Comparative International Budgeting and Finance (1984)
(editor, with Jesse Burkhead)

*Aspectos del Presupuesto Público (1988)
(editor, with A.L. Antonaya)

*Government Financial Management (1990)
(editor)

*Public Expenditure Management (1993)
(also in Russian)

*Published by the International Monetary Fund

A. Premchand

Effective Government Accounting

International Monetary Fund
Washington, D.C.
1995

This book was designed and produced by
the IMF Graphics Section

Library of Congress Cataloging-in-Publication Data

Premchand, A., 1933–
    Effective government accounting / A. Premchand.
        p.   cm.
    Includes bibliographical references.
    ISBN 1-55775-485-3
    1. Finance, Public—Accounting.   I. Title.
HJ9733.P73   1995
350.72'31—dc20   95-17823
                                                                       CIP

Price: US$21.00

Please send orders to:
International Monetary Fund, Publication Services
700 19th Street, N.W., Washington, D.C. 20431 U.S.A.
Tel.: (202) 623-7430   Telefax: (202) 623-7201
Internet: publications@imf.org

For Nikhil,

Neeraj, and Indu

Preface

Although government accounting has existed for more than two millennia, it has not received its due. In fact, accounting has been looked down upon and viewed by nonusers as a set of archaic rules that have long since ceased to be relevant or effective. Yet, in addition to governments, ordinary citizens and democratic institutions charged with legislative oversight must contend with government financial accounts and related systems of accounting. There is recognition that these systems stand to be improved, and, from time to time, commissions are appointed to look into improving them. They conduct a debate on the subject, recommend changes, and go through the motions of implementing the changes, with no visible impact on the perceptions of the public or on the operations of those involved in the enormous and growing amounts of paperwork that constitute government accounting.

More recently, owing to the fiscal stress that many governments have experienced, the content, form, and organization of government accounting have received renewed attention. This time, there is hope that the focused attention and the public debate may have a more enduring impact on the future course of government accounting.

This book attempts to shed light on the processes and problems of government accounting and on how the discipline may be revitalized. It recognizes that this reform is too important to be left to government accountants alone but requires the concerted efforts of administrators, commercial accountants, economists, and, most important, the public.

In a way, the book represents the author's views, knowledge, and memories acquired as participant-observer in more than three decades of national and international civil service. The experience gained in the process was refined through regular exchanges with academics, accountants, and administrators in a number of countries.

In an earlier form, the book was discussed in detail at a seminar sponsored by the IMF, the European Union, and the United Nations Development Program and held in Accra, Ghana in November–December 1994 for senior officials of 17 African countries. The views of these officials have been taken into account in the preparation of the book for publication. An earlier draft of the book was read by Adolf Enthoven, Richard Bird, Richard Goode, Andrew Likierman, and Y.V. Reddy, and their comments and criticisms have proved invaluable. It was also read by several of the author's colleagues in the Fiscal Affairs Department of the IMF and was reviewed, in detail, by a team of senior officials from the U.S. General Accounting Office. Their comments have helped in refining the content. As always, the author alone is responsible for any errors that may remain.

The preparation and publication of a book are occasions for incurring more debts of gratitude. The author is grateful to all the individuals named above, who unstintingly gave him the benefit of their views, and to David Driscoll and Jagdish Narang, who were supportive through the book's preparation and publication. He is also grateful to Hildi Wicker, who typed the different versions of the book, and Elisa Diehl of the External Relations Department, who edited the book with care and craft.

Contents

Introduction

This study is an attempt to delineate the role of accounting in the fiscal management of nations. Its fundamental premise is that accounting has a crucial role in the formulation and implementation of fiscal policies and indeed lies at the heart of modern governments. To grasp its significance, its nature, tasks, and evolution have to be explained.

Evolution

Over the years, accounting inevitably developed in various ways in different milieus. While no effort is made here to provide a history of the developments in accounting, recognition of five stylized stages in its growth and application may be in order. These five stages also indicate that each one of them left an indelible impression on the content of accounting in governments. First, the earliest references to accounting in Western societies are to be found in the practices of the governments in Athens and in the Eastern societies, in the practices of kingdoms in China and India and in the pre-Christian era. These developments, which were more or less contemporaneous, emphasized the recording of transactions and developed reporting and inspection systems, as associated features, with a view to ascertaining the status of the finances of the monarchy. For example, in China, the emperor himself heard reports delivered by officials on changes in population in different regions, changes in cultivated land, and records of transactions of receipts and disbursements of money and grain. This system was utilized to determine whether the records correctly reflected the real situation of the population and property and to safeguard royal property from internal fraud. Kautilya, a prime minister of a kingdom in India, wrote more than two thousand years ago that the "king shall have the work of heads of departments *inspected daily* (emphasis added), for men are by nature fickle and, like horses, change after being put to work. Therefore, the king shall acquaint himself with all the details—the officer responsible, the nature of the work, the place of work, the time taken to do it, the exact work to be done, the outlay and the profit." The primary task of accounting as the record of the king's finances continued for centuries, less as a science and more as a practice that evolved from changing need.

The second stage reflects an organized attempt to codify the system. Although double-entry bookkeeping evolved about five hundred years ago, it had little impact on accounting in government, which remained a bookkeeping operation, devoid of theory or methodology. This attempt was made by the cameralists of Germany, who dominated the thinking in regard to royal finances from the middle of the sixteenth to the end of the eighteenth century. Their approaches sought to strengthen the position of the ruler and contributed to attempts at systematizing the administrative routine of fiscal departments. An inevitable consequence of their efforts was the extensive centralization of financial management and verification as the primary means of control. These very features later became the major issue between the royalty and the paying public.

By the nineteenth century, as the public came to acquire more control over the purse and exercised this control through well-established parliamentary routines, the tasks of accounting also grew. In this third stage, while the old theme of providing information about government finances continued, this time it was to a different master, reflecting a shift from the crown to the representatives of the public. The accounting system began to be specified in laws and statutes, and the records maintained in the government acquired legal sanction. The laws also specified the respective duties of the crown, the legislature, central agencies, which were primarily responsible for the day-to-day tasks of control, and the spending agencies. This type of legislation continues to be in force in several industrial and developing countries, and some of the recent legislation enacted in a number of countries has its origins in the laws enacted during the nineteenth century. As colonialism spread, the practices of the metropolitan governments also extended to the colonies. Thus, the practices in Great Britain spread to its colonies in Asia and elsewhere, and the French practice and practices of other European countries found their way to their respective colonies. In the process, even contiguous countries came to have different systems that reflected their different colonial origins and regimes.

In the fourth stage, accounting began to reflect the changes in the nature of the economic regime and the expanded scope and much diversified and complex nature of the tasks undertaken by governments. The advent of centralized planning in the Soviet Union brought with it both a change in the tasks of government and, consequently, its accounting systems. Although governments traditionally undertook massive investments in public works and in the establishment of railway and transport systems and waterworks, their role as investors received a substantial boost in the context of centralized economic planning. While government accounting became somewhat secondary in the overall scheme, and statistical systems gained ascendancy, the scope of accounting systems also expanded to deal with assets and liabilities in the world of quasi-commercial transactions of governments. The accounting system had to contend with costs of production, appraisal of investments, and a host of related activities.

From this, the movement to the fifth, or current, stage was only natural. As the scope of government operations grew, budgets acquired new and deserving prominence as instruments of public policy. Economic planning was expected to strengthen the role of the state as producer, while budgets became the main tools of distribution and stabilization. These functions and the growing massive interaction between government and the community also implied that if budgets were to be successful as instruments of policy and economic management, they had to be ably served by accounting. As fiscal policies became more calibrated in the pursuit of economic stabilization, accounting became more important as a reporting system with measurement of the receipts and expenditure and their implications. As a system (which the *Shorter Oxford English Dictionary* (p. 2115) defines as "a set or assemblage of things connected, associated, or interdependent, so as to form a complex unity; a whole composed of parts in orderly arrangement according to some scheme or plan"), accounting is charged with identification, selection and analysis, measurement, estimation, processing, and communication of information on receipts, expenditures, assets, liabilities, costs, and benefits, and all other aspects that legitimately form part of fiscal management. Accounting now is the recognized handmaiden of fiscal policy.

Despite its long pedigree, government accounting has suffered a benign neglect at the hands of the accounting profession and the government. For too long, the issue for the accounting profession was whether government accounting was different from the accounting system of other kinds of entities and, if so, in what way. The general notion that accounts of an entity should provide records to meet three different groups of needs was also deemed to have applicability to government organizations. Thus, all accounts should conform to the statutory and associated legal requirements that specify the content of records and the type of information to be generated. Those records should also meet the requirements of stewardship, and, thus, the needs of the groups external to the management of the entity regarding the evaluation of the entity's performance are to be recognized. Within the entity, management also needs regular information to enable it to perform its functions efficiently and effectively.

It was held that these general principles have varying applicability to the government. The laws specifying the accounts may have more extensive legal requirements in governments, reflecting in turn the separation of financial management functions between the legislative and executive branches of government. There may also be substantial differences in the structure of funds between entities and government. In one sense, the term *funds* means resources, and in another, it represents an accounting entity. It is this aspect that is of crucial importance from the point of view of financial control. In government, there may be several funds—general funds, special funds, debt-service funds, foreign aid funds, trust funds, enterprise funds, capital project funds, earmarked funds, and so on. Similarly, governments have been obliged to maintain budgetary accounts reflecting the record of appropriations, releases, commitments, payments, and uncommitted balances. These accounts reflect the budgetary structure and are intended to provide a continuous tracking of events as they occur. In general, governments have not been obliged in the past to maintain proprietary accounts regarding assets, liabilities, income, expenditure, and net worth.

In all these areas, developments over the years have had a major impact on the course and tenor of financial management and therefore on accounting in government. The range of functions undertaken by governments, particularly in the development, social, and enterprise sectors, has grown rapidly in size. As these developments have not been anticipated by the laws, the laws have become obsolete. Furthermore, government accounting has been immensely influenced by changes in technology. More important, the changing tasks of macroeconomic management have imposed new demands, in addition to the traditional management needs, on the accounting system. The accounting systems in government should now reflect changing patterns in public expenditure management.

Recent Changes

The worldwide fiscal stress experienced during the past decade and a half has induced a greater awareness of the need for doing more with fewer resources. This in turn has unleashed substantial efforts to (1) expand the range of techniques of control; (2) improve the overall administrative context within which controls are operated; and (3) bring about appropriate institutional changes and improvements. Research conducted during the period has shown that the success of controls is less dependent on the ownership factor than on the methods of control utilized and the administrative or corporate culture within which they operate. Recognition of this factor and the acute fiscal problems brought about simultaneous developments in the above three areas.

A brief description of these developments, including their features and limitations, and related issues is in order here. Three preliminary considerations, however, need to be kept in view.

First, the expenditure control framework, whether exercised by the executive branch, the legislature, or independent audit agencies, has four basic elements—policy controls, process controls (covering release of funds, monitoring, contract monitoring, and payment controls); regulatory controls (including specification and oversight of accounting standards); and efficiency controls (including ex post evaluation by the audit agencies, where applicable). Of these elements, developments in process controls are discussed in some detail here. (Regulatory aspects are discussed in Chapter 3.)

Second, a major objective of controls is to reconcile the often divergent needs of the policymaker at the macroeconomic level with those of the program manager in the spending agencies. Far too often, both by tradition and as a result of the prominence of macroeconomic goals, the needs of macro managers are emphasized at the expense of the needs of micro or program managers. Now, however, there is greater and explicit recognition of the needs of the microeconomic level as well as an acceptance of the need to deliver services within the framework of specified resources. In this context, accountability is larger in scope and includes, in addition to the rendition of accounts of moneys collected and spent, the results achieved. As such, macroeconomic goals, while having an undeniably pre-eminent role in the policy framework, would have less viability if they were to be achieved at the expense of delivery of services.

Third, controls are, to a very large extent, influenced by developments in public sector management as a whole. The experience of several countries shows that recent efforts have aimed at introducing a new managerial outlook into government. This outlook emphasizes results over processes, flexibility over conformity, judgment over compliance with routine, innovation over risk aversion, and overall organizational development of institutions so that they could become productive and well performing. The efforts of Australia and New Zealand in "strengthening" their public sector, of Canada in its "initiative for Public Service 2000" (popularly known as PS2000), of the United Kingdom in the "Next Steps and Citizens' Charter," "Fundamental Review of Running Costs," and "Better Accounting for the Taxpayer's Money," of the United States in "reinventing" government, and of Italy in its "reorganization proposals" initiated in 1993 all represent facets of this new outlook. The new managerial outlook includes specification of standards and measures of performance, emphasis on output controls, greater competition in the public sector, and more focus on discipline and economy in resource use. All these features aim at helping managers to manage. These in turn imply that controls can no longer follow traditional centralized command-style methods but must give more financial power—and accountability—to managers.

Objectives of Control

Control techniques are not intended to be applied in a mechanistic fashion but to meet specific objectives, including the following:

- Economy, efficiency, and program effectiveness in the use of budgeted resources.

- Resource use that will promote economic stabilization. To the extent that some issues have not been adequately addressed during the budget formulation stage, or to the extent that there have been major economic developments that indicate changes in the course of policies adopted, they will need to be suitably addressed by ex post controls.

- Adequate accountability in the delivery of services—not merely for the resources used, but for overall performance, including courtesy in the delivery of services.

- In all the above objectives, the framework of controls should permit transparency in the implementation of government policies.

In the past, accounting and transparency have received relatively little attention. However, in the quest for greater citizen participation and for a more accountable government, they have acquired a justifiable importance of their own. Recent emphasis on governance or reinventing government is no longer a matter of academic or political debate, but has become an integral part of the everyday consciousness of the citizen.

Range of Process Controls

As noted earlier, controls range from the release of funds to the closing of annual transactions and related accounts. These controls have undergone, or are undergoing, changes in the ways described below.

From Fund Controls to Global Budgets

The traditional goal of controls is to regulate the flow of funds to the spending agencies, primarily through a system of "time-sliced" releases of funds (for example, quarterly apportionments). In the current context of increased decentralization of responsibilities and greater autonomy to program managers, the regulation of the flow of funds needed to be supplemented with additional control mechanisms. The evolving system has four elements that form the basis for controls and that do not impinge on the operational autonomy of program managers: global budgets; specification of required outputs; delineation of standards of service; and determination of costs for certain major categories of services, whether delivered directly by government or by contractors.

Global budgets imply a departure from conventional line-item budgets and represent an implicit contract for the provision of services from given resources. In this framework, the central agencies are responsible for ensuring a smooth flow of budgeted resources while the spending agencies are responsible for providing services. Control is transformed in the process from a narrow mechanism for regulating cash flows (which, under the new system, would be the primary responsibility of the agency) to a broad one based on the nexus of physical and financial flows that would, inter alia, permit a much needed emphasis on outputs.

Global budgets, unlike traditional budgets, are not limited to technical compliance with the budget estimates. They have a more important task—the delivery of services. Specification of the quantitative and qualitative aspects of these services is, therefore, an essential part of the new government financial management approach. While the qualitative aspects of services still need to be developed and refined, the new approach has already contributed to an improved functioning of controls. In several cases, particularly in the provision of medical care, cost data have been developed for various types of illnesses, and hospital budgets and related reimbursements (when services are provided by nongovernmental organizations) are linked to these standards. This technique recognizes that what cannot be measured also cannot be captured by the control system—hence, the emphasis on measurement.

From Cash Limits to Cash Management

In the mid-1970s, cash limits came into greater use as one way of restricting outlays in an inflationary context. It was recognized then that indexation had an inherent problem in that it was difficult to finance the constantly increasing outlays because of linkages to the cost of living or other indices. Cash limits provided a more effective instrument because they represented limits beyond which governments were unwilling to neutralize the impact of inflation, and spending agencies had somehow to adjust their activities within these limits. However, where expenditures were dominated by transfers and entitlements, the range of activities within the purview of cash limits was limited. Furthermore, the system became one of backdoor budgeting, whose allure was lost with the introduction of global budgets. This view, however, should not be interpreted as a denial of the merits of cash limits, which can be useful as a short-term instrument for bringing some order in an inflationary context.

In the new context of decentralized tasks and responsibilities and global budgets, greater importance is being given to cash management. Although it is by no means a new technique, it acquired additional importance for the macro manager charged with implementing a budget. It is now recognized that budget allocation of resources, always a difficult task requiring the best of diplomatic skill, is only a beginning. It needs to be supplemented by techniques that seek greater convergence between revenue inflows and expenditure outflows so that borrowing and the burden of interest payments can be reduced. To achieve this purpose, governments are now required to avoid immobilizing resources that agencies are permitted to retain, to prepare schedules for bulk or heavy payments so that the call for borrowed resources can be anticipated, and, generally, to minimize uneconomic borrowing either from the market or from captive resources. Where interest payments range from about 20 percent to 30 percent of total outlays, the importance of cash management cannot be overemphasized.

Responsibility for cash management, once shared with central banks, is now largely the function of the ministries of finance. It is a responsibility that is no longer perceived as a "reactive" approach to the spending patterns of administrative ministries and agencies but as a "proactive" policy

stance that needs to be formulated on the basis of the balance between resource needs and resource availability during budget implementation.

Policy Reviews

While important, control techniques have proved to be less than adequate in dealing with mandatory budget outlays, which exacerbate the
deficit (however measured) if the shortfall in revenue is greater than expected. This outcome is fairly common in several industrial countries,
which, in the course of implementing budgets, recognized that the revenue forecast was based on optimistic assumptions, while expenditures
were estimated to be growing conservatively. A way had to be found to
link revenue and expenditures, particularly where the latter are dominated by mandatory payments.

The U.S. Budget Enforcement Act of 1991 sought to specify such a link
between revenue and expenditures. For this purpose, outlays were divided
into three categories, and increases in some were to be adjusted against reductions in others or alternatively through additional mobilization of resources (the "pay-as-you-go" process). The law envisaged a detailed
sequestering process that would automatically be triggered if deficit limits
were about to be exceeded. However, under the best of circumstances, it
affects no more than 3 percent of outlays, because certain categories of expenditure (for example, interest payments and wages and salaries) are ex-
empt from sequestration. Nevertheless, the law is useful because it forces
a reconsideration of the laws relating to certain large outlays.

Another systemic development that forces such a policy review, at both
the budget formulation and implementation stages, is the problem of financing government contingent and unfunded liabilities, including pension payments. These liabilities are often not recognized during the budget
preparation phase nor in the rough and tumble of the budget process.
Now, however, a number of governments have accepted the need for introducing a commercial type of accounting that recognizes payables, contingent liabilities, and unfunded liabilities and requires their measurement.

Evaluation

Generally speaking, problems experienced during budget implementation stem from formulation. Addressing such problems at a later stage may
not produce the hoped-for results. This raises the question of whether

preventive action can be taken, for it would have a more enduring impact than the curative action. It is with this in view that evaluation of completed programs and projects was initiated as an ex post control but with an impact that transcends the budget implementation phase. The evaluation consists of an assessment of progress and its impact, so that areas of success and failure in implementation can be identified. It is a distinct process aimed at examining the program rationale, achievement of objectives, cost of achievement, and exploration of alternatives. It seeks to analyze the program objectives so as to assess the viability of the targets, examines the organizational adequacy for implementing the assigned tasks, evaluates the impact through an analysis of the flow and distribution of benefits, and identifies how staff, materials, and money are used.

Evaluation is not new and indeed has been a part of the financial manager's lexicon for more than four decades. It has acquired a new urgency, however, as the traditional avenues for controlling expenditures have been yielding fewer results than expected. Evaluation, as current experience indicates, can have at least three forms. First, it can be incorporated into the budget formulation stage, as has been done in Sweden. The Swedish triennial budget system is, in effect, a mandate for a systematic and intensive evaluation of about one-third of the Government's activities every three years. Second, evaluation can be undertaken for completed programs and projects by the administrative ministries, as is done in Canada and Germany. Here the methodology of evaluation is specified by the central ministries and the evaluation results are utilized to improve resource use and allocation. Third, evaluation can be conducted by an external audit agency.

The results of evaluation may not be dramatic in terms of their impact on the implementation of an ongoing budget. Their value lies, to the extent that public organizations are willing to learn the lessons of experience, in their ability to prevent a recurrence of past patterns of policy implementation. Although evaluation is also viewed as a tool for ensuring accountability, it serves primarily to link formulation and implementation and is used by the executive.

From Financial to Efficiency Audit

The role of the external audit agency has also changed in recent years. A quick review of existing audit practices in industrial countries suggests three types of governmental audit: (1) a comprehensive audit of the financial statements of the government, or the public sector in some cases, with a view to certifying compliance of laws and examining efforts to secure economy, efficiency, and effectiveness in the use of budgeted resources; (2) a quasi-judicial approach with the objective of determining the adequacy of the law, examining infractions of the law, and determining penalties. This approach also includes the preaudit of expenditures to ensure compliance; and (3) investigations into special issues, coupled with efforts to ensure that the accounting systems in the spending ministries and agencies and related internal systems are adequate for their purposes. Some audit institutions may follow a combination of these approaches, but the primary function in most cases is likely to be one of these types.

Traditionally, ex post controls were conceived in terms of an annual, financial audit by an independent statutory agency that consisted in commenting on the compliance of legislative appropriations and the patterns of their use. Over the years, there has been extensive discussion about whether the audit agency should also undertake an efficiency audit. Although there were several issues concerning the measurement of efficiency, they were largely overcome in countries where the financial management system had been transformed into a decentralized one with specific work measurements and performance yardsticks. In this context, the extension of the audit agency's functions from a financial audit to an efficiency audit or, as popularly known, a value-for-money audit (covering economy, efficiency, and effectiveness) was natural.

The value-for-money audit is not confined to ensuring economy but is intended to examine and report on the results achieved. The audit agency is expected to identify ways of improving efficiency and assist the government in taking necessary action to improve systems and controls. It broadly supplements the internal evaluation system described earlier.

The value-for-money audit does not question the merits of policy objectives. Rather, it is concerned with the means and techniques of policy implementation, recognizing that the primary responsibility for securing value for money lies with the spending agency. The role of the audit in this case is to provide an independent examination of how far and how well that responsibility has been discharged. To the extent, however, that lessons of experience are always valuable, it assists in the formulation of future policies.

Involvement of the Users

Recently, some local governments in the United Kingdom have begun to associate the users with their operations. As a part of this initiative, user groups are involved in formulating service agreements and in defining the scope and quality of services to be delivered by the local government. Service contracts provide a direct cycle of accountability between the elected members, management, staff, and users (and back again). It is seen as more effective than adding to the already costly supervisory layers of management. It provides a powerful stimulus for the management to be more vigilant in providing services and to evaluate those services from the users' point of view. This experiment, if successful, is likely to be widely emulated.

Institutional Development

Controls, whether ex ante or ex post, imply a hierarchical relationship where one agency is endeavoring to influence or change the policies or operational approaches of another. Experience shows that when such controls are exercised in a centralized or inflexible fashion, they may have an adverse impact on the financial responsibility of the spending agencies. The major issue of control has thus become one of reconciling the needs of central agencies with those of spending agencies, and of exercising those controls so that they promote financial responsibility within the agencies. This issue has been approached in two ways during recent years.

The first approach involves providing incentives to spending agencies for procuring economies in expenditures. It recognizes that even if the control framework is effective, more could be obtained by providing incentives to spending agencies. It implies that the knowledge of operations and their financial implications is to be found in the first place in the spending agencies, which are therefore best placed to explore the possibilities for economies. In Australia, for example, spending agencies were allowed to retain a share of the economies they secured to use on approved programs. This approach provides a refreshing departure from the traditional controls. While such incentives are likely to yield declining results in the medium term, the approach offers yet another avenue that, when judiciously implemented, could have a far-reaching and enduring impact on the financial responsibility of spending ministries.

The second approach relates to organizational development. This approach looks beyond the scope of the control framework and aims to make the organization more effective and thereby more responsive. The Office of the Auditor General of Canada has made a number of efforts to address this issue. (Its studies *Constraints to Productive Management* (1983), *Attributes of Well-Performing Organizations* (1988), and *Values, Service and Performance* (1990) examine the ways in which organizations in government could be made more effective.) These efforts point to the need for greater decentralization, specification of standards, flexibility in resource management, accountability for results, and adaptability for changing needs. In turn these features are expected to contribute to a more effective organization.

The range of developments discussed here offer considerable potential for pursuing economy, efficiency, effectiveness, and stabilization goals in the management of public expenditures. Experience shows that not all the developments are to be found in all the industrial countries. Rather, each country is endeavoring in its own way to absorb and apply these new approaches. But even as the approaches are being implemented, criticisms are being leveled against them. Some point out that they use methods inspired by private sector practices that are not entirely suitable to the operations of the public sector, where decisions tend to be made with an eye to the political rather than to the financial implications. Others argue that the new approaches may lead to the emergence of a new system that will not necessarily be as productive as claimed. Some suggest that the claims of benefits are exaggerated.

Some of these criticisms are premature. In assessing the ability of the new techniques to reduce expenditures, some critics may not have fully separated the impact of economic cycles on expenditures. Clearly, the new techniques must be implemented for an extended period of time before a detached appraisal can be made. Recent experience further underscores the traditional point that the task of improving governmental organization is never complete. It is a continuous effort that affords no respite to the fiscal policymaker. The promise of any reform can be realized only when the reform is sustained by relentless zeal and unflagging effort.

Some government financial managers tend to take the view that existing control systems are adequate. They attribute the failure to achieve the control objectives to policies, politicization of governmental decision making, and a lack of well-trained personnel. The issues discussed here show that, in evaluating the adequacy of the control framework, a government must begin by distinguishing those aspects that can be controlled and those that may be outside its immediate purview. Such an inward look is likely to reveal the antiquated organizational and management structures, unsuitable operational computer technology, and poorly designed regulations and other weak mechanisms that abound in government.

In sum, governments at all levels are expected to be more responsive, accountable, and cost effective. The new tasks have come at a time when there is much dissatisfaction with the existing systems, particularly with their inability to make payments or furnish reports on time. These tasks and related expectations suggest that it would be unrealistic to expect major successes from fiscal policy unless the supporting institutions are adequately strengthened. In this regard, accounting, which has a high impact in all the above areas, plays a major role and therefore needs to be addressed in a substantive way. Cosmetic reforms, which may have quick appeal for short-term political purposes, would hardly serve the purpose and may even be damaging in the longer term. An essential step is therefore to analyze, in each case, the issues and the options available for addressing them. The experience of countries that have made pioneering efforts will provide particularly valuable information.

In the following chapters, an attempt is made to examine the major aspects of government accounting, starting with payments and concluding with the rendition of accounts. Each chapter considers historical developments, features of existing systems, and recent advances and their adequacy relative to the current and future tasks of governments. Consideration is given to institutional linkages with other types of accounting used for analytical purposes, and particular attention is paid to the role of technology. An interdisciplinary approach is adopted so that the role of government accounting in the overall framework of macroeconomic management can be considered in proper perspective. The intent is to evaluate the state of the art and, in doing so, to facilitate the formulation of an agenda for strengthening accounting in government. In each area, answers will be sought to the following questions: What are the tasks? How are they being performed? Are there any issues? Are they conceptual, organizational, or technological? How can improvements be made? Do those improvements imply substantial changes? How can the transition be managed?

1

Payments Systems

Traditionally, the literature on accounting and central banking has viewed payments systems in government as a mechanical process. Consequently, scant justice has been done to systems that bring the government closer to the taxpaying public.[1] For the purposes of this analysis, accounting is viewed as a system with two primary purposes—to organize all procedures connected with the receipt and disbursement of funds to and by the government, and to organize bookkeeping so that these transactions can be recorded in a transparent manner that will allow full disclosure of the financial status of a government entity. Payments, either to or from the government, represent the first operational stage in the financial management process of the government but should not be viewed as a purely internal process of the government. The growth of central banking and the associated development of clearing arrangements have reached the stage at which they need to be considered in conjunction with the linkages between the central bank and the government. Indeed, the improvements that a government can make in these payments systems are dependent on the level of development of the banking payments system. In addition, gradual improvement in the application of computer technology and related electronic processing has opened up new vistas, and organizations and systems that were hitherto considered essential are now being reviewed to determine if they are viable in the new context. There is, moreover, a perennial need to make the operations cost effective and user friendly. These considerations suggest that payments systems have entered the mainstream for accountants, expenditure managers, and central bankers—reason enough to consider the various aspects of the systems. The chapter therefore considers first

---

[1]Literature on accounting in general, and government accounting in particular, pays little attention to payments systems and related issues. Even literature devoted to descriptions of expenditure management pays no attention to these aspects. For illustrations of this type of literature, see, for example, Organization for Economic Cooperation and Development (1987), or the United Nations, Economic and Social Commission for Asia and the Pacific (1993). None of the country profiles included in these studies provides any description of payments systems in operation. For a review of the literature and related aspects of the role of payments systems in central banking, see Summers (1991).

the distinction between accounting and payments systems and later deals with the payment processes, organization, modes of payment, relationships with the banking system, and financial reporting. The concluding section is devoted to a consideration of the interenterprise arrears that have emerged during recent years as a major issue in the economies in transition.

Payment Stages

As indicated earlier, it is appropriate that the government accounting system be considered in a broad perspective inclusive of the payments system. For the sake of precision, however, the numerous stages involved in the process may be enumerated so that the payment stages can be distinguished from the technical accounting stages. The steps on the expenditure side are given below.

(1) Record of budgetary appropriations.[2]

(2) Record of budgetary allocations to the various agencies.

(3) Maintenance of records of commitments.

(4) Collection and verification of payment claims.

(5) Issue of instructions for actual payment.

(6) Record of payments made.

(7) Record of goods and services received.

(8) Record of goods and services actually used by the agency in the provision of a service.

There are similar stages in the payments received by the government.

(1) In regard to taxes, assessments may be made by the government or, on a self-assessment basis, by the taxpayer.

(2) On the basis of the assessment, payments are made at specific intervals, either to the tax agency or through the post office or a depository financial institution.

(3) Documentation of the payment made is sent by the taxpayer to the government. The government may also receive confirmatory evidence from the place where the payment is made.

---

[2]In some countries, the appropriation process referring to legislative approval may not obtain. Rather, a decree implying the highest level of authority is issued indicating the amounts available to each agency.

(4) On the basis of the above evidence, action on the claim against the taxpayer is completed.

(5) Similar procedures may be in operation for the payment of fees and other interagency payments.

The tasks of payment refer to (5) and (6) on the expenditure side, and to (2) and (3) on the receipts side of the operations of the government. Stages (1) and (2) on the expenditure side are viewed by some as more of an integral part of budget implementation, while accounting is viewed as being concerned with (3), (4), (7), and (8). For analytical purposes here, budget implementation is viewed as the initial phase of accounting, where the emphasis is more on the release of budgetary authority to the agencies than on the agencies' actual spending. In regard to tax collection, however, practices vary among countries, but the assessment and collection of taxes due are generally considered the legitimate tasks of the tax administration machinery.

Release of Funds and Organizing Payments

Although payments may represent the penultimate stage in the financial management process of a government, this stage is preceded by numerous checks and balances, all of which are intended to prevent the misuse of funds. The first step in this process relates to the release of funds provided for in the budget. In this regard, as well as in regard to the other steps discussed below, there are several variations in the practices of countries. The attempt here is to consider the broad patterns rather than the specific practice in one country. The first variation relates to the distinction between the release of budgetary authority and the release of budgeted funds. In most governments, the rules specify that no expenditure can be incurred without the specific approval of the ministry of finance or the treasury, as it continues to be called in several countries. But approaching the ministry of finance for approval for each item of expenditure could lead to an administrative gridlock. To avoid such an untenable situation, the ministry of finance delegates financial powers to the controlling officers to encumber the budgeted funds and to pay them at a later stage. Without this authority, the agencies cannot initiate action for spending their budgets.

As soon as the budget is approved, the authority to incur encumbrances and to spend the amounts is conveyed to the agencies. Such budgetary authority may be conveyed for specific categories of expenditures, while for others the ministry of finance may continue to exercise authority centrally. In some countries, the transfer of budgetary authority is followed by the release of funds provided for in the approved budget. Because governments do not have all the funds needed for the purpose at the beginning of the year, they are compelled to release funds on a time-sliced basis. Even the time-sliced release may not totally prevent strain on those engaged in the country's cash management, particularly when the budget deficit is significant.

Three types of practices for releasing funds exist. The first type refers to the countries in which budgeted amounts are available soon after the budget is approved. In a few British Commonwealth countries (such as India) and in some of the economies in transition, the budgeted amounts are available to the agencies for commitments and spending from the onset of the fiscal year. In a few other countries, releases are made on a routine monthly basis for current outlays, while more ad hoc procedures are followed for the construction budget. Some of these countries have since moved to a system of time-sliced releases in the context of fiscal austerity and a more intensive search for instruments to ensure compliance from the spending agencies. A second arrangement is one under which formal warrants (called *exchequer issues* in technical parlance) are issued by the ministry of finance in response to requests from the spending agencies. Such requests have no defined periodicity and primarily reflect the changing seasonal requirements for outlays other than those on personnel. Under a third type of arrangement, fixed amounts are released for commitment and payment on either a monthly or a quarterly basis.

All these arrangements regulate the release of budget authority rather than amounts of cash to be credited to spending agencies. In some countries, such as the Philippines during the early 1970s and the Islamic Republic of Iran, actual amounts are released, which may then be credited to the accounts of the spending agencies. When the spending agencies maintain these amounts and related accounts as a part of the consolidated pool of money used by the government, the impact of this procedure on cash management is minimal. When these amounts are maintained as a part of deposit accounts of the spending agencies maintained with commercial banks, the procedure has an adverse impact, and the government would be hard put to maintain its own liquidity except through more borrowing. Countries may not follow these procedures consistently for their current, capital, and development budgets. Releases for development budgets, for example, may be ad hoc and are governed, in most cases, by the action plans submitted by the major project authorities.

The question arises as to whether these three types of releases have different implications for control. The question may appear to be somewhat redundant in the current context of information and telecommunications technology, which has made data available more or less instantaneously as transactions occur. The release of budgetary authority through a warrant was a procedure meant to fulfill one of the pillars of parliamentary accountability. As legislative control evolved, the need arose for an independent authority to look into the claims of the spending agencies after the approval of the budget. For this purpose, a paymaster general was appointed in some countries, while in a few others the approval of the audit authority (in most cases a formality performed with a total lack of zeal, and a procedure that continues largely because of a lack of interest in revamping what has become essentially a routine in search of a purpose) was also needed.

The time-sliced release of spending authority was, however, derived mostly to reinforce the controls exercised by the ministry of finance. From the ministry's point of view, several policy measures are included in the budget without adequate examination, and some are included on the specific condition that no commitments would be made in regard to these proposals until they are reviewed and approved by the finance ministry after the start of the year. In addition, the needs of cash management (that is, to bring about a convergence, as far as possible, between inflows and outflows so that borrowing may be organized in the best possible manner in the circumstances), as well as the need for major adjustments in fiscal policy in the event of a resource shortfall, have contributed to a strengthening of this type of control exercised by the ministry of finance.

It could be argued, however, that some of these controls are largely academic and are less effective than they appear to be. Further, they may also adversely affect the sense of financial responsibility in the spending agencies. More than 95 percent of governmental outlays are of a continuing nature, and the bulk of them go for personnel, interest payments, entitlement benefits specified by legislation, and projects whose implementation is spread over several fiscal years. In such circumstances, the share of outlays that can be adjusted annually may be very small. Besides, the seasonality of these outlays should be familiar to those engaged in cash management. In such a context, the exercise of control is viewed as a tyranny of the central agencies over the spending agencies. Moreover, attempts by the central agencies to control the activities of the spending agencies are likely to reduce the financial responsibility in the latter. In an age when the canons of managerialism argue in favor of greater decentralization and endowment of responsibility in operational agencies (so as to ensure a balance between responsibilities and related power), the exercise of any additional check by the finance ministry or the central budget office is viewed as avoidable. This view is buttressed by data-sharing arrangements that suggest that every action, regardless of size and impact, can be monitored by the central agencies. If commitments are known, then payment lags can be estimated. It is thus argued that full responsibility should be given to the spending agencies from the beginning of the fiscal year.

The other side of the coin is that the central agencies require windows of opportunity in the overall expenditure management process to enable them to fulfill their responsibilities for the macromanagement of the economy. The release of budgetary funds is only a preliminary step in the larger process, and its effectiveness will be assessed in conjunction with other steps. This leads us to consider the other stages of control and the role of the finance ministry in each of those phases.

Commitment Stage

In several countries, spending agencies are technically free to make commitments for the policies and projects for which amounts have been allocated in the budget. This procedure is based on the belief that requisite planning and fulfillment of specified regulations have already taken place. In practice, however, there are several elements on which action remains to be taken, and, inevitably, the central agencies become involved before commitments are made. This is particularly the case when major projects are funded by external aid and when international competitive bidding is obligatory. In such cases, the central agencies are also included in the tender committees responsible for the award of contracts. This permits the spending and central agencies to track the developments at every stage.

In the French type of treasury systems (as well as in its variants, such as the Italian system), the spending agencies are expected to obtain approval for each proposed commitment from the treasury representative attached to that agency. This practice not only ensures compliance with the laws and regulations, but also facilitates cash management so that the lags between commitment and payment can be ascertained and adequate arrangements made where bulk payments are involved. In the former centrally planned economies, there was no need to obtain the approval of the central agencies at the stage of commitment. There is now, however, a gradual movement toward monitoring of commitments by central agencies, an effort that is facilitated by the availability of a general ledger system maintained by computers. This system shows the various stages in the spending process, including commitments made and their legal status, in considerable detail.

Types of Payments Systems

A "payments system" is defined as one that "includes all the decisions and actions that are involved in making payments with government funds for government activities."[3] The payment process involves two components: a review of the claim for payment and associated documentation and the actual responsibility for payment. The mode of payment, which is also an important element, is discussed below.

The review is intended to ensure that the proposed payment is legal, that requisite funds are available and have been properly provided for in the budget, that the officer authorizing or approving the payment is indeed the official so designated for the purpose, and that what is proposed to be paid is indeed the right amount for the purpose. Every government official bound by the common code of conduct and ethical behavior is expected to honor this in his or her day-to-day official business. Traditionally, however, the officials of the spending agencies have been viewed as lax in this regard, and their actions therefore need to be monitored by the ministry of finance.

This practice has its origins in the old kingdoms, where special cadres were developed to protect the wealth of the king. Kautilya, the Indian philosopher-statesman, wrote more than two thousand years ago that "just as it is impossible not to taste honey or poison that one may find at the tip of one's tongue, so it is impossible for one dealing with government funds not to taste, at least a little bit, of the king's wealth." He added "just as it is impossible to know when a fish moving in water is drinking it, so it is impossible to find out when government servants in charge of undertakings misappropriate money."[4] To prevent misap-

---

[3]United States, Treasury Department (1989a), p. 4.

[4]See Kautilya (1992), pp. 280–83. He further noted that "it is possible to know even the path of birds flying in the sky but not the ways of government servants who hide their (dishonest) income."

propriation, procedures were developed so that each claim could be verified by more than one person before it was paid. Procedures now in vogue in many countries have their origin in this desire to protect the wealth of a country by involving many officials so as to prevent collusive behavior. Indeed, in several countries, payment vouchers must be signed by more than one person. This verification process is the cornerstone of expenditure control in a number of countries, including some in the industrial world. The final step in this approach is that checks for higher amounts are signed by the ruler himself—a procedure that is found in some Middle Eastern countries even today. Over the years, it has contributed to some distinct practices. In the United States, each payment must be certified by the certifying officer who is attached to an agency.[5] Similarly, in the French and Italian systems, payments must be reviewed by the official of the ministry of finance attached to each agency.

The existing arrangements for review and payment in several countries fall broadly into four categories.[6] First, where the responsibility for the documentation and related payments is vested with the spending agencies, the involvement of the ministry of finance is limited to the preparation of the budget and thereafter to the time-sliced release of budgetary authority and funding. The practitioners of this type of approach include China and the United Kingdom. A second type of arrangement is one in which the spending agencies are provided with specialized personnel under the control of the ministry of finance to help the spending agencies manage their payments processes. The responsibility remains that of the spending agencies, but financial matters are administered by cadres maintained by the ministry of finance. For purposes of day-to-day control, however, they are managed by the spending ministry. This approach is prevalent in India and a few African countries.

The third type of arrangement is one in which an exclusive agency, generally a part of the ministry of finance, is responsible for payments. This system had its origins in the days when banking facilities were extremely limited, and all collections and disbursements, including those in outlying areas, were made by officials of the trea-

---

[5]Different types of outlays have different requirements. Third-party payments in Russia, for example, which primarily related to food procurement from agriculturists, are made by the branches of the Bank of Russia on the basis of submission of documentation relating to the delivery of grains.

[6]Many of these aspects are illustrated in Table 4 of the modules included in Appendix I in Premchand (1993), pp. 208–61.

sury.[7] Even with the spread of the banking system, however, the treasury system continued, and in some countries, such as France, the treasury also began to accept money deposits and thus performed selected banking functions primarily with a view to reducing its own debt costs. This type of treasury system, where all payments must be approved and paid out by the representatives of the ministry of finance, continues to this day in several countries.[8]

In a fourth type of arrangement, payments for certain transactions are managed by a single agency at the center, regardless of where the transaction occurred. Within this broad framework, however, there are individual nuances and variations in each country. For example, with the development of technology, some payments are being made on a centralized basis, largely for reasons of convenience, such as payroll administration. In some countries, the payroll is administered either by the personnel ministry or by the ministry of finance, and payments are made to the staff through a computerized system.

The basic issue in the design of payments systems is who should be responsible for preparing the requisite documents (on the basis of which a payment is made) and for making payments—that is, who should be responsible for signing checks. The answer may be somewhat straightforward in that the two responsibilities should be integrated and performed by the same agency. The agency that is responsible for preparing the documents should be responsible for payments, too, and the converse of this proposition (the one that is responsible for payments should also be responsible for the documents) is equally correct. As an extension of this logic, it could be argued that separating these functions has the potential of contributing to a loss of financial responsibility in the agency charged with preparing the documents and may thus contribute to an avoidable

---

[7]In some contexts, the term *treasury* often denotes collection and payment responsibilities. In practice, the term also has a broader connotation. Thus, ministries of finance in several countries are known as the treasury—as in Australia (which also has a ministry of finance), New Zealand, Sri Lanka, Tanzania, the United Kingdom, and the United States, among others. In view of the lack of precision in the use of the term and with a view to avoiding possible confusion about the intent in the use of the term, it is more appropriate to use neutral phraseology, such as *government payment system*. This broader approach would facilitate the inclusion of all types of financial transactions, including foreign aid, that may be in forms other than cash. Noncash transactions may not pass through the treasury, which generally is more concerned with cash inflows (or other forms of banking) and outflows.

[8]There may be notable exceptions to this, however. In the United States, social security payments are directly made by the Social Security Agency, and health care payments are made by a separate agency. Also, payments of interest on securities are made by the Federal Reserve System. All other payments are made by the certifying officers attached to various agencies.

dyarchy. Also, an integrated management could contribute to a reduction in the overall costs associated with the payments system.

In an opposing view, the separation of payment responsibilities may be, and often is, justified on the grounds that the spending agencies cannot be trusted to manage funds, that it is necessary to ensure legal compliance, that it facilitates cash management by the ministry of finance, and that such an arrangement provides a degree of professionalism in the conduct of public affairs. A more detailed examination of these views suggests that they may not be fully tenable in the current context. Governments have grown so big that centralized financial management may not be viable. Besides, the argument that spending agencies do not have financial consciousness is at best rhetorical and may be unfounded. Legal compliance is as much a matter for the official in the spending agency as it is for others. Moreover, available evidence in many countries suggests that slippages occur in payments even when administered by the agencies of the ministry of finance. This compromises the role of the paying agency as well. In reality, this issue has never before been examined in this objective fashion. Rather, most of the arrangements that are now found in many countries are largely the legacy of convention and laws whose validity in the computer age remains to be proven.

The advent of electronic data processing has led to changes—for example, regardless of who makes the payment and where it is made, legal compliance can always be assured. Cash management requires up-to-date information and not centralized management. An appropriate analogy is that of an automatic traffic control system and the role of a traffic controller. If the system is available, the only role for the latter is as backup and monitor of the traffic flow. There may then be no need to post a traffic controller at each intersection. In much the same way as the introduction of technology changed the fundamental equation between the central agency and the spending agencies, issues should be reviewed and the systems redesigned to be cost effective.

Method of Payment

There has been a phenomenal change in methods of payment in recent years. Traditionally, in its early stages, the banking system conducted all inflows and outflows in cash. Later, as the banking system evolved, greater use was made of checks, and, with the application of electronic technology, greater use is now being made of electronic cards and transfers. The range of instruments now being used by most countries is illus-

Table 1. Payment Methods (Excluding Foreign Aid)

Cash	In several countries, particularly the former centrally planned economies, payments to and by the government are made in cash. One of the primary responsibilities of the ministries of finance in these countries is to ensure that every payment office has adequate cash. During periods of hyperinflation, provision of cash tends to be a difficult exercise. Cash also continues to be the predominant medium in some Middle Eastern countries, despite the availability of banking facilities.
Checks	Several countries accept checks (for payment of taxes and related levies) from the public and also make payment through the issue of checks or payment authorizations, as they are sometimes called. Payroll, pensions, debt repayment, and payment for centralized procurement of stores typically take the form of checks issued on either the central bank or commercial banks.
Book adjustments (or nonpayable checks)	Government departments are often required to make payments to other departments that provide common services for the government as a whole. In such cases, book adjustments are made from the budgetary allocations of one department to the allocations of another department. As these book adjustments involve the maintenance of suspense and exchange accounts that, in turn, become cumbersome and contribute to long—but avoidable—delays in the final consolidation of accounts, they have yielded place to the issue of nonpayable checks or central adjustments by the finance ministries.
Electronic card payments	Payments of certain taxes (e.g., customs duties) as well as payment for procurement of specific categories of stores or equipment are made through electronic card transactions.
Electronic transfers	This method of payment, which is heavily dependent on the available computer terminology, is undertaken in lieu of the issue of checks. It is considered more cost effective and secure than the methods described above. (A good example of the electronic transfer system was the Social Accounting Service of the former Yugoslavia, which worked as a clearinghouse and settled more than two-thirds of budgetary transactions through electronic transfers.)

trated in Table 1. Table 2 shows the methods used for the transmission of foreign aid. Table 3 illustrates the range of payment instruments now in use in one of the advanced industrial countries—the United States.

Experience shows that the transaction costs of cash payments are labor intensive and are therefore the most expensive method of payment, while electronic transfers are the least expensive. Payment through organized channels such as the banking system require that the payee have a bank account. Some, however, are reluctant to transact through the bank-

Table 2. Foreign Aid Transactions

Technical assistance	Whether provided as a loan or as a grant, this takes the form of personnel (both bilateral and multilateral) placed at the disposal of the recipient government to be utilized according to an agreement. As salaries are paid by the donors, these transactions do not pass through the payments systems of the recipient government unless part of the expenditure must be met in local currency.
Cash grants	These transfers, whether made by individuals or by public bodies, are expected to pass through the government payments systems and be counted as receipts and expenditures.
Grants-in-kind	These may take the form of food or equipment and, in either form, may not pass through the government payments system except where counterpart funds are generated and subsequently credited to the account of the government.
Import support program	The World Bank and regional financial institutions have been extending import support program loans to several countries. In such cases, the counterpart proceeds of imports are transmitted through the government payments systems.
Direct provision of equipment	Where loans are given to governments, the specific project authorities receive equipment for their projects directly from the suppliers selected on an international competitive bidding basis. The suppliers are then paid by the international financial institution on the basis of documentation furnished by the suppliers. These transactions are not normally recorded in the government payments systems.
Reimbursement	The recipient government makes purchases (as part of a loan agreement) by advancing its own resources, which are then reimbursed by the donor on receipt of the requisite documents. There is generally a lag between submission of a claim and its reimbursement. However, several financial institutions have established revolving funds to minimize the delay.

ing system because they consider it to be not particularly user responsive, more so in countries where all banks function as a part of the nationalized sector. Others trust the traditional methods and are wary of the risks associated with banking, such as insolvency, and a few others appear to prefer cash transactions because they can avoid detection by the tax authorities.[9] During recent years, however, with growing reliance on the banking system, checks have come to be a significant method of

---

[9]It is estimated that in the United States about 80 percent of all retail transactions are paid in cash, although, in terms of value, the proportion is much smaller. See Pingitzer and Summers (1994), p. 108.

Table 3. Range of Payment Instruments Used in the United States

Types of Instruments	Features
Payments by the Government	
Cash	Payments are made in the form of cash by authorized personnel. Although this instrument has high flexibility and global acceptance, increasingly, the share of payments made through cash is declining.
Government bank card	This is a commercial bank card issued to designated officials to make small purchases. This reduces the need to maintain small amounts of cash, and the banks are reimbursed for purchases made.
Debit card	This is primarily used by imprest holders to replenish their imprest funds by drawing from an automated teller machine (ATM). Obviates the need to issue separate checks and related paperwork for the replenishment of the imprest.
Diners Club card	This card, which is based on a competitively awarded contract, is intended for the use of federal employees to cover transportation and related expenses. The employee makes the payment to the issuing bank and is reimbursed for expenses incurred. Reduces travel advances and associated paperwork.
Direct deposit	This method allows the employee to have salary and other payments directly credited to his or her account. These transactions, which take place through an automated clearinghouse,[1] are usually made through the electronic funds transfer (EFT) system.
Electronic funds transfer	This term is used to identify delivery systems to transfer funds electronically rather than through paperwork. The transfers are made through computer, magnetic tape, plastic card, or telephone.
Fedline	This is a communication channel maintained by the treasury with the federal economic system that facilitates the transfer of funds to financial institutions.
Fedwire	This is a facility operated by the Federal Reserve System to facilitate interbank transactions. Participating banks (not the government) use it to run daylight overdrafts, which they are required to clear by the end of the day.
Fiscal agency checks	These are issued by the Federal Reserve System on behalf of the treasury (Bureau of Public Debt) for payments related to public debt securities.
Government travel system	This is a part of the Diners Club card and is a centrally billed account (on a monthly basis) primarily for the issue of travel tickets. Full information is provided by the billing company, on the basis of which reimbursement is made. The billing itself is done through a magnetic tape.

Table 3 (*concluded*)

Types of Instruments	Features
On-line payment and collection system	This is a component of the overall on-line accounting link system and is used for interagency billing and adjustment through a telecommunications network.
Treasury financial communications system—letter of credit	This is an electronic funds transfer system that provides advance financial commitments to organizations performing contract work for the federal Government.
Treasury checks	These refer to payments authorized by designated officials and are issued in the form of checks from a payment voucher submitted to the treasury in response to a request from an agency.
Treasury third-party drafts	This is an alternative payment mechanism for agency imprest fund transactions and is paid by the issuing agency rather than by a financial institution.
Vendor express	This is specifically designed to facilitate payments to vendors, who are expected to maintain corporate accounts at financial institutions. Payments are made electronically on the expected date through the clearinghouse network.
Fiscal agency checks	These are issued only by the Federal Reserve Bank when securities are presented on their maturity. These checks are issued in lieu of cash payments.
Zero balance checks	These checks are drawn on commercial banks, which accept them as cash items, and are primarily used to expedite payments in disaster areas. It is a checking account that maintains no balance.
	Payments to the Government
	In addition to cash, check, and electronic transfers, the following facilities exist:
Lockbox	The lockbox network is intended to accelerate the deposit of funds to the treasury's account. Under this system, remitters mail their payments to a specific post office box where the designated bank picks up the mail and sends it to the treasury. These include retail, wholesale, and electronic lockboxes.
Treasury tax and loan payments	These may be made through 15,000 financial institutions throughout the country.

Source: United States Treasury Department (1989a).
[1]The automated clearinghouse is a central distribution and settlement point for transferring funds electronically between two depository financial institutions.

Table 4. Volume of Noncash Payments Handled by Type of Instrument, 1992[1]

(In percent)

Country	Checks	Credit Transfers	Direct Debits	Payment Cards
Belgium	18.8	56.8	8.8	15.6
Canada	62.4	4.4	4.3	28.9
France	50.8	15.4	10.2	15.0
Germany	8.8	49.8	39.3	2.1
Italy	40.0	42.1	4.1	3.7
Netherlands	12.3	61.3	23.8	2.6
Sweden	8.9	77.7	4.6	8.8
Switzerland	4.4	81.3	2.5	11.8
United Kingdom	45.0	21.0	15.0	19.0
United States	80.5	1.8	0.9	16.8

Source: Bank for International Settlements. Reproduced from Pingitzer and Summers (1994).
[1]Totals may not add up to 100 percent as there are other types of payments not included here. It should be noted that these reflect economywide transactions and not those of government payments.

payment. Increasingly, electronic transfers are becoming more significant in many countries, as may be seen from Table 4.

In fact, the improvement of the payments system is viewed now as one of the major tasks of central banks[10] and of the banking system. Electronic systems not only reduce the cost of operations[11] but also bring change to the organizational culture. There is more effective use of computers and telecommunications, and many stages of paperwork that were routinely involved in cash and check payments are compressed and carried out in a shorter time, giving operational officials more time to address other issues.

A review of the payments systems in many countries shows a few areas that need to be addressed so as to make them user friendly as well as efficient. It is generally alleged that the systems in many countries take a long time to process payments, with the intended recipient often employing additional people to chase the paperwork and obtain payment. The costs incurred in the process are necessarily included in the contract quotations submitted to the government, thus increasing its costs. In some

---

[10]Some central banks routinely devote a part of their annual reports to describing the efforts being made to upgrade the payments system. See Banca d'Italia (1992), which emphasizes the importance of efficiency and security integration (pp. 130–35).

[11]The recent report by Al Gore calculated that electronic transfers cost only 6 cents a transaction compared with 36 cents a check (Gore, 1993a), p. 113.

cases, payments are so delayed that vendors have stopped providing services to the government except in exchange for cash, a process that adds to the transaction costs. However, in some cases, advance payments contribute to avoidable borrowing costs. In others, payments to outlying areas are considerably delayed, particularly in the transition economies (mostly in Eastern Europe), which have poor banking facilities.[12] (For this reason, post offices are extensively used in several industrial countries, including Italy, Sweden, the United Kingdom, and the United States, to make payments in outlying areas.)

It is therefore essential that payments systems be reviewed to ascertain which administrative stages can be compressed and which delivery mechanisms can be made more efficient. Such efforts are being made, even without advanced technology, in countries such as Botswana and Oman. In Botswana, all government utility bills (for example, for water, electricity, and telephones) are centrally paid out by the ministry of finance, which then deducts the amounts from the budgets of the respective agencies. A similar practice is found in Bahrain. In Oman, vendors are permitted to maintain accounts with the Central Bank of Oman, which makes payment on electronic advice from the Government by transferring funds from the Government to the vendors. These experiences suggest that inexpensive approaches can be devised even within the existing institutional framework.

The general experience of a cross-section of countries shows that more than 60 percent of government payments occur at the national headquarters of the government or, in a federal setup, in regional or state headquarters. This percentage tends to be higher where the bulk of the annual budget outlays are devoted to interest and entitlement benefit payments. Although some of the beneficiaries, particularly those that receive entitlement benefits, undoubtedly live outside the capital city, it would be appropriate to take advantage of the available banking facilities to introduce more efficient methods of payment. Apart from reducing costs, this would pave the way for a greater acceptance of electronic transfers. For the remote areas, however, conventional methods of carrying cash imprests or third-party drafts continue to be valid, although their share in total payments will gradually decline. Proposals to introduce electronic transfers raise the question of whether this method entails greater security risks than conventional methods.

---

[12]Folkerts-Landau, Garber, and Lane (1994, p. 94) observe that "in most Central and East European countries, interbank payments are so sluggish that there may be delays of as much as several weeks during which neither payee nor payor has access to the funds. This results in widespread use of cash, which is less convenient and secure in other respects."

Security of Payments

Traditionally, the safekeeping of funds received and held for payments has been one of the main considerations in the physical design of the treasury office. Before the introduction of cash, precious metals and jewelry as well as taxes paid in kind (a share of the produce) were all retained in the treasury office. In his treatise, Kautilya even provided an architectural design for the storage of these materials.[13] (He specified that the commodity warehouse and granary should be in a brick building, above ground, with many rooms on all four sides surrounding a covered quadrangle on two rows of pillars and with one entrance.) Later, with the introduction of money, treasuries were designed with built-in safes and a 24-hour protective force.

In more recent years, however, with depository institutions holding money, traditional treasuries have essentially become centers for processing payments. One exception is Viet Nam, where one of the main functions of the treasury is the safekeeping of money, and relatively less reliance is placed on the banking system. Most treasuries now have computer terminals, and more efforts are devoted to maintaining computer records at the required temperature than to ensuring the physical security of the office itself. (Here, again, there are exceptions. For example, in Italy, the computer processing center of the government accounts has been fortified to withstand terrorist attacks.) By and large, however, concern about physical security has substantially abated in light of the fact that most money is kept in banking institutions.

Slippages, fraudulent payments, and embezzlement are constant concerns despite the transformation in the way in which transactions are carried out. Rather than decreasing because of computerization, irregular payments and embezzlement now require professional skills. These problems, and the methods for avoiding them, may be broadly stated in the following way. Fraudulent payments and embezzlements occur when the maintenance of the records is inadequate (either by design or by accident) and oversight is found wanting. To avoid these problems, traditional methods of control rely on verification at several points in the process, so that each step can be reviewed in the following stage. But this has proved to be too expensive and, in terms of results, counterproductive, and the increased paperwork has contributed to higher transaction costs. Several checks and balances have been introduced

---

[13]See Kautilya (1992, pp. 216–20). Although available archaeological evidence does not show whether this design was indeed implemented, Kautilya was both a practitioner and a prime minister. It may thus be expected that such treasury offices were indeed built.

into the design of computerized processing as a result. These are relatively quick, accurate, and inexpensive. In any event, the need for the proper maintenance of accounting records and regular inspection can hardly be overemphasized.

A common problem relates to forged checks, which, in some countries, have become an unintended cottage industry. The result invariably is a considerable loss of revenue to the government. To tackle the problem, some countries have taken steps to require those responsible for issuing checks to inform banks of the checks' serial numbers so that only authorized payments can be made. The same can be applied to computer processing, but centralized issue of checks would require, as a precedent, a good telecommunications technology. The computerized system is also designed to create a full electronic trail to show how the payment is organized, reviewed, approved, and, finally, implemented. These steps ensure that legal and regulatory requirements are fully met and that, when any changes are made, they have been fully authorized and controlled. Even so, computers are designed to carry out a large number of transactions (such as interest and benefit payments) automatically, and it may not always be possible to verify individual transactions.

Relations with the Banking System

As noted at the outset, the efficacy of the government payments system is in part dependent on its relations with the domestic network of banking institutions and their operations. The government's relationships need to be analyzed in terms of those with the central bank and with the commercial banking system. In many countries, the popular belief, often shared by government officials, is that government is responsible for raising and spending funds and that any gap that results from this process should be financed by the central bank. This lends credence to the view that the central bank works mostly at the behest of the government and that any constraint it seeks to impose becomes a soft one. In fact, however, the constraint, as indicated in the respective legislations of the central banks, would appear to provide for a hard one. Features of the legislation are described for some industrial countries in Table 5. It shows that there is a wide variety of transactions between central banks and governments in that advances, overdrafts, and other credits may be made available either on mutually agreed terms or on terms specified by the central banks.

Table 5. Central Bank and Government Transactions: Practices in Selected Industrial Countries

Country	Practice
Canada	The central bank may buy and sell securities issued or guaranteed by Canada or any province.
	The bank can make loans to the Government of Canada or a provincial government. Such outstanding loans should not at any one time exceed one-third of the estimated revenue of the Government of Canada and should not exceed one-fourth of a provincial government's estimated revenue. These loans are to be repaid before the end of the first quarter after the end of the fiscal year during which the loan has been contracted. The terms of these loans are determined by the bank.
France	The central bank maintains the treasury's current account without any charge.
	The bank participates, without any charge, in the issue of loans and securities by the treasury.
	The Government can obtain loans and advances from the bank on terms and conditions mutually determined and approved by Parliament. In addition, the Government can get an overdraft of up to F 20.5 billion at no interest.
	The bank may discount, acquire, and sell securities, but the treasury may not present its own bills for discounting by the bank.
Germany	The bank may grant short-term advances in the form of book credit and credit against treasury bills to the federal and Laender Governments subject to limits (which are periodically changed). No charges are made for these advances. The bank may decide as a part of its policies not to rediscount treasury bills and securities issued by the Government.
Italy	The bank engages in the investment and discounting of securities issued or guaranteed by the state.
	The bank is also authorized to provide advances equivalent to 14 percent of the estimated expenditures of the Government at a rate of interest of 1 percent. This provision has since been repealed.
Japan	The bank may make advances to the Government without any collateral.
	The bank buys and sells government bonds and obligations.
	The bank manages treasury funds.
Netherlands	The bank acts as a depository of the treasury without charge.
	The bank acts as cashier to the Government.
	The bank may be required, under instructions, to make advances to the Government against sufficient security, free of interest. Such advances are not to exceed f.150 million at any one time.
	The bank buys, sells, and discounts treasury bonds.
Switzerland	The bank buys, sells, and discounts treasury bonds.
	The bank accepts and makes payments on behalf of the confederation and maintains the Federal Debt Register. These activities are undertaken free of charge.

Table 5 (*concluded*)

Country	Practice
United Kingdom	The bank, as fiscal agent of the Government, receives and makes payments.
	The bank buys, sells, and discounts treasury paper.
	Remuneration to the bank for services rendered is jointly determined by the bank and the Treasury.
United States	The Federal Reserve buys, sells, and discounts federal bonds, bills, and securities.
	The Federal Reserve used to extend advances of up to $4 billion to the Government but no longer does because the relevant law was not renewed.

Source: Compiled primarily from the legislation governing the central banks. The table is based on legislation prior to 1994. In some cases, such as France and Germany, changes have been made to conform with the Maastricht Treaty.

Historically, the amounts of such advances and overdrafts have been determined as a share of government revenues or expenditures. But in the member countries of the European Union (EU), these features have changed or are being changed to conform with the provisions of the Maastricht Treaty. Article 104 of the treaty prohibits the provision of overdraft or any other type of credit facility by the central banks to central, regional, local, or other public authorities. The central banks are also enjoined, under this provision, not to purchase directly any debt instruments issued by governments.

A similar review of developing countries shows that in about half those surveyed, the central bank is prevented from providing overdraft facilities to the government and that substantial caveats govern when it may provide credit.[14] Although the role of the central bank as a fiscal agent of the government covers a number of areas, for the discussion here, three functions are relevant: (1) as a banker to the government; (2) as a provider of credit, albeit within limits, to government; and (3) as an agent responsible for maintaining the public debt register and related transactions. The process and its implications as well as related issues are considered below.

Traditionally, governments have deposited their moneys with the central banks. The initial rationale for this approach could have been the proximity between the government and the bank as well as the perceived security inherent in the situation. With the growth of commercial banking, the question arose as to whether some or all of the deposits could

---

[14]For a review of these aspects and related issues, see Leone (1991), and Cottarelli (1993).

be maintained with the commercial banks. However, because of apprehension that large government deposits could contribute to credit creation and that movements in these deposits could destabilize the commercial banks and their operations, this change was slow to gain acceptance. It is now recognized that in large countries these dangers may have been overstated when the money markets and the interbank markets are well established and are functioning smoothly.

In small countries where interbank market facilities are practically nonexistent, maintaining government deposits with commercial banks could pose avoidable problems. Maintaining all government deposits with the central bank, apart from facilitating liquidity management (not to mention the accounting convenience), could also contribute to more effective monetary management. It should be noted parenthetically that in about 80 percent of the countries surveyed in a study conducted at the International Monetary Fund, the government is allowed under law to keep deposits outside the central bank.[15] In several cases, however, this is viewed as enabling legislation rather than as actual practice.

The provision of credit by the central bank to the government is a more complex process and is best examined in terms of formal or legal aspects and informal relationships. Because the central bank functions as the main depository of government funds, the government is entitled to certain advances and credit from the central bank (see Table 5), which fall into eight broad categories:[16]

(1) Net outstanding cash advances to the government should be zero at the end of the fiscal year.

(2) While no explicit limits are specified, provision of credit may require the approval of the legislature, the government, or the central bank.

(3) No limits are specified, but the circumstances under which advances may be made and the purposes for which they may be made are stated in the relevant legislation.

(4) No explicit limit is specified.

(5) A limit is indicated as an absolute amount in domestic currency, usually as a part of annual financial legislation by the legislature and may thus be revised from time to time.

(6) A limit is established in the form of a proportion of the central bank's liabilities.

---

[15]See Cottarelli (1993), p. 9.
[16]Extracted from Leone (1991), p. 364.

(7) A limit is established as a percentage of government revenues.

(8) A limit is established as a percentage of government expenditures.[17]

These provisions of law are intended to provide safeguards and protective barriers to the central bank's management. In practice, however, the picture may be different, and when government borrowing is substantial, banks may be pressured to circumvent the laws. The experience of a cross section of countries shows that government relationships with the central banks have the following features: First, in many countries, the rates at which credit is provided are often lower than the market rates, and a lenient treatment is extended to governments. Second, where the legal provisions deal with the stock of credit as a percentage of revenue or expenditure, governments manipulate the credit limits in their favor. Third, where limits exist on central bank credit, governments use the financial intermediaries that have access to central bank credit to borrow from it and lend it to the government. Fourth, in many countries, central banks on-lend foreign financial resources to the government in domestic urrency and at low interest rates. The terms of lending are so generous that the brunt of adjustment, in the event that credit or exchange rate risks materialize, falls on the balance sheet of the central bank, inevitably contributing to its losses. Furthermore, when substantial foreign exchange losses occur, governments, particularly those that have hard legislative constraints, appeal to the central banks for financing.

Notwithstanding all the laws discussed earlier, these appeals are heeded. Effectively then, the quasi-fiscal accounts of the central banks end up as extended arms of government operations. Finally, where limits exist, the technicality of compliance becomes an issue. Are these limits to be observed throughout the year or at specific times, such as at the beginning or end of a month, a quarter, or a fiscal year? Although continuous compliance is both legal and prudent, in practice, compliance is tied to a specific point in time. The intent of the limit, specified in any manner, is to induce the government to estimate its resources (including credit) regularly and manage them effectively so as to avoid any transgression of limits. However, expediency gains the upper hand, and compliance may be nominal, without the requisite adjustment in expenditures and related payments.

---

[17]These limits are on a gross basis and are exclusive of the deposits maintained by the government with the central bank. It is sometimes argued that the limits should be on a net basis. Such a provision would enable the government to get large amounts of money by maintaining a balancing deposit and thus defeats the very purpose of limits.

In some countries, uncashed checks have become a major problem. In these countries, spending agencies issue checks as and when they are due. But central agencies, recognizing that there is not enough money to cover the checks, instruct the central banks informally not to make the payments. This phenomenon could be viewed as the result of the aggressive policies and postures of the governments or the lack of independence of the central bank and suggests that the informal network between governments and central banks differs fundamentally from the one envisaged in formal and legal relationships. The resolution of these issues lies not only in giving more independence to the central bank but, most important, in improving the expenditure management and payment processes in the government.

Commercial Banking

The importance of the banking system in the overall framework of government payments has grown with the decline of transactions in cash. Although in several countries cash transactions are still dominant, very few countries continue to operate independent treasuries while relying less on the banking system. Even in countries in which the role of the treasury was, and continues to be, to receive and make payments, cash transactions have declined, and greater reliance is placed on payments through checks and related instruments drawn on depository financial institutions. The broad range of relationships now existing between government and the banks is illustrated in Table 6. In the first category, the borders between the government and the banking institutions are ill defined. Checks issued by the government are honored by the banks regardless of the availability of balances, for the simple reason that banks are owned by governments. There may be no formal organized channels of lending to government. On the other side, the banks stand to benefit in that the revenues they receive are not transmitted immediately to the government account. This delay (which is to be found even in industrial countries, such as Italy, where the banks normally retain the taxes they collect for about three days before transmitting them to the government) works in favor of the banks, which, therefore, prefer to provide this function to providing services for a fee to the government, which would oblige them to surrender immediately the taxes they collect. This kind of relationship obscures the reality of short-term financing of the budget. Moreover, the retention of funds by banks for longer periods works against the interest of the government when inflation is high and may

Table 6. Relations with the Banking System

All-in-the-family syndrome	In some countries, the commercial banking system, or at least part of it, is owned by the government. In these cases, selected commercial banks are specified for receiving as well as for making government payments. In the event that outflows exceed inflows, the gaps are covered from the resources of the banks, frequently without any charge. The banks also hold government deposits on which no interest may be paid. Moreover, revenues collected by banks may not be transmitted to government accounts for extended periods. In some cases, budgetary allocations are released to the credit of the spending agencies at the beginning of each time slice. Thus, for all intents and purposes, banks are considered as a part of the extended family of the government.
Specialized banks for specific purposes	In many transition economies (including Algeria, China, and Viet Nam) specialized banks—agricultural development, industrial development, communications, and transportation— are established and the related sector ministries are expected to channel their payments through these banks. Usually, budgetary authority is transferred to the credit of the ministries in the accounts held with the banks.
Revolving funds with selected banks	In some countries, a few banks, regardless of ownership, are selected to receive and make payments. Although some of the services are provided free of charge, banks are compensated in other ways (e.g., revolving funds may be maintained by the government on which no interest is paid by the banks). Payments made by banks are immediately cleared with the central bank so that the levels of revolving funds may be maintained. Further, revenues received are transmitted to the central bank without delay.
Regular commercial transactions and payment for services rendered	In some countries, banks function as collection and payment agencies for revenues and expenditures. In addition, some of them have agreements for financing electronic card payments. In these cases, revenues are transmitted to the government soon after receipt, and payments made are claimed through the clearing process.

even contribute to greater deficit financing. However, when banks are not owned by the government, but function independently, the relationships are commercial and, thus, transparent. This type of relationship (fourth category in Table 6) accepts the traditional distinctions between government and the banking system, and all transactions are aboveboard. Even recent instruments such as electronic card purchases are awarded to commercial banking institutions on the basis of competitive bids and have an assured integrity.

The second type of relationship has been a common feature in the economies in transition. Although some of these countries have wound up the operations of these specialized banks in light of their recent commitment to move toward a market economy, they continue to operate in, for example, Algeria and China. In China, all receipts flow into one account maintained at the People's Bank of China (central bank), while payments are made through 23 independent and separate accounts that the Government holds at the same bank. The surpluses in some accounts cannot be used to compensate for deficits in other accounts, thus contributing to the rigidity of the system. For specific expenditures like capital construction (general) and capital expenditure for agriculture, payments are made through three specialized banks: the Bank of Construction, the Agriculture Bank, and the Industrial and Commercial Bank.

Elsewhere, governments maintain revolving funds (to cover payments for a week) with selected banks. These banks make the payments and, with a view to maximizing their own earnings, arrange to clear their claims quickly. The banks may not be rewarded for the services provided. In addition to commercial banks, post offices are used extensively to make mostly low-value payments in rural areas. These transactions are carried out through giro payments, which in effect are payment orders that allow funds to be placed to the credit of a specific beneficiary. The post offices may be given advances (to meet high pension outlays that usually occur at the beginning of the month) or their claims may be resolved through the normal clearing system. Giro payments can and are used for both recurring and nonrecurring transactions.

Three broad issues arise in connection with payments: the need for efficiency, the resolution of excessive check float, and the politicization of the payments process. The need for efficiency stems from a variety of considerations. First, an efficient system reduces the cost of operation and uncertainty to the payers and payees. The technical efficiency of the payments system influences the efficiency with which the stock of money balances is used in the banks, as well as the way in which cash management is organized in the government. Cash management aims at arranging greater convergence between inflows and outflows throughout the fiscal year so that the strain on borrowing can be reduced. Partly, both these aspects depend on the clearing arrangements in the economy.

In recent years, some countries have made concerted efforts to improve clearing arrangements both internally and for cross-border transactions. While the introduction of electronic technology has permitted the development of several quick modes of payment, in the final analysis, the clearing system should have well-defined standards for operational reliability. The government payments system is increasingly dependent on this reliability (as are all others who transact through the banking system), as the clearing system represents the apparatus through which cash balances are transferred and by which credit is extended. These issues are, however, more within the realm of central banking and are therefore not taken up here for any detailed consideration. It is important to reiterate that the ability of the government to pursue its policies of macroeconomic management depends partly on the efficiency of the payments system. It is therefore necessary to examine the approaches and issues discussed earlier to determine their current status and the steps necessary to improve the efficiency of existing payments systems.

Checks are debit instruments and those issuing them enjoy the advantage of a float for the time it takes a check to clear the banking system. It is argued that this type of float "rewards the payer with what amounts to an interest-free loan, and tends to impair both the efficiency and safety of the payments system."[18] While part of the solution lies in the way in which paperwork is organized in the paying institution as well as the controls exercised by the central agencies, the issue can also be addressed in part through the application of available technology. Check processing is now highly automated in several countries that use a truncation approach under which documents are stopped at the point of first deposit (or at a later point), and relevant information for collecting the check is captured and converted into electronic form, after which the funds are paid out quickly. This type of technology is now readily available and it would appear that latecomers do not have to traverse the same route that other countries have. To the extent, however, that checks are issued far in excess of balances and their payment is therefore kept pending at the central bank, more concrete measures may be needed in the expenditure management process itself. Such an issue of checks is a symptom of lack of financial discipline in the government and must be addressed as such.

It is frequently alleged (and there is adequate evidence in support of this allegation) that banks are subjected to severe political pressure by governments to make payments even when there are no balances—a practice that has contributed to commercial bank losses. In effect, this implies that commercial banks have become instruments for carrying out the policies of the government. It is suggested that pressure to pay is ex-

---

[18]See Pingitzer and Summers (1994), p. 110.

ercised primarily in the interior of a country where the influence or the discipline of the ministries would appear to be weak. Two suggestions have been made to address this problem. One is to strengthen the role of the commercial banks and to empower them to reject payments when there are no balances. This, however, is by no means a new approach. Indeed, it is a part of the standard prudent behavior that a bank at a minimum is expected to follow. Nonobservance of this precept has given rise to the current problems.

Second, it is suggested that a treasury system be reinstated to act as a disciplining force between the check-issuing authority and the commercial bank. It may be recalled in this context that some countries abandoned the traditional treasury systems as the banking system became more efficient. The spending agencies were given enhanced financial powers to issue checks and make payments through direct arrangements with the banks.[19] The reintroduction of the treasury would mean an expansion of the process, an increase in costs, and a curtailment of the responsibilities of the spending agencies. Those who favor reintroducing the treasury system suggest that treasuries would not only scrutinize payments but would be responsible for compiling accounts. But such a step could widen the chasm between expenditure responsibility and the power of payment. Moreover, experience shows that treasuries are no less resistent to political pressures than are the commercial banks. Circumvention and politicization cannot be cured through the reintroduction of the treasury system. Rather, observance of discipline, which is an essential part of effective government financial management, must be secured through tighter controls, periodic oversight, strengthened accountability, greater citizen participation, and, above all, greater transparency.

Financial Reporting

The detailed components of financial reporting and organizational implications are discussed in Chapter 6. This section is concerned only with payments and the reporting of payments to the spending and central agencies. When payments are made through the banking system, daily scrolls of inflows and outflows are reported either to the spending

---

[19]The checks paid out by the commercial banks are usually further scrutinized by the central banks before they are cleared through the normal arrangements. It occasionally turns out that the checks paid out are fraudulent, in which case the commercial bank must assume responsibility.

agency or to the designated organizational unit of the ministry of finance. On the revenue side, these scrolls indicate the amounts received and from whom they are received as well as the dates of the transactions. On the expenditure side, they indicate the payments made, to whom they are made, and related details. These daily—in some cases weekly—scrolls do not present the data by budgetary category but only show the chronological sequence of transactions regardless of the purpose and amount. Because these data are based on actual amounts paid out, they tend to differ from those maintained by the spending agency, which are based on checks issued. The discrepancy between the two indicates the size of the float.

In countries that have a traditional treasury system, reports are compiled showing the transactions conducted during a specific period. There may not be any float in cases where the agency is responsible for issuing the payment order as well as for the actual payment. Reports may show only the sequence of transactions and the aggregate flows, which the spending agency then reclassifies in terms of the budget categories.

Although timeliness, coverage, and classification have traditionally been the principal problems associated with financial reporting, countries with on-line computer systems can now maintain and update records as transactions take place. Moreover, relevant data are available to the spending agencies (for their micromanagement) and to the central agencies as well as the central banks (for macromanagement) simultaneously, eliminating many problems that used to arise in this area.

Interenterprise Arrears

Interenterprise arrears have recently become a serious problem in many countries that are in transition to market economies, for example, in the former Yugoslavia during the early 1980s and in Viet Nam during the late 1980s. Enterprises were being liberated from centralized controls, provision of credit, and marketing and were expected to function autonomously guided by market forces. During the early 1990s, interenterprise arrears increased rapidly in some countries and again became a major problem. For example, in Russia, these arrears amounted to about Rub 48 billion at the beginning of 1992 and, by mid-1992, had grown to over Rub 3 trillion, or twice the value of domestic credit. This enormous growth suggests that many firms that would otherwise have ceased to function were getting an extended reprieve by being allowed to build up arrears. They were also contributing to a decline in tax revenues, despite high levels of inflation, largely because taxes were assessed on the basis of financial transactions recorded through the banking system. Because arrears contribute to large lags in registration, they exacerbate the already critical resource situation of the government and can destabilize the economy as the implied credit expansion and tax avoidance intensify inflation. The arrears may be the result of a policy failure (including a failure to anticipate and monitor the widespread resort to escape mechanisms by the management of enterprises), a failure of the payment system, or a combination of the two. To determine the cause, the nature of the arrears and the factors that contributed to them must be examined.

Although common in many countries, interenterprise arrears tend to become a major policy issue in countries that have large public sectors. In these economies, working capital is generally supplied, at the instance of a central directive, by the central bank or another specific bank, as part of the development plan. They are also tied in large measure to the transfers from government budgets, and when this regime is changed and the banks stop providing credit, then enterprises are faced with three options: to find credit elsewhere, to close operations, or to incur arrears to the suppliers. Enterprise managements tend to choose the last approach as an escape mechanism. But when most or all enterprises resort to the same mechanism, the intent behind the change in the policies stands to be defeated.

During periods of high inflation, enterprises whose prices continue to be determined by the government tend to build up receivables (which are arrears for other enterprises), which grow. In addition, during a recession, enterprises that do not have the flexibility to adjust their scale of operations may also build up arrears, as they must use the limited moneys they have to pay wages and salaries. Besides, when as a part of anti-inflation strategy, less credit is made available, then the enterprises build up arrears. Specifically, in the Russian Federation, two factors contributed to interenterprise arrears. First, there was a substantial cash shortage from 1992 until the newly independent countries introduced separate currencies.[20] This contributed to a situation under which the Russian Federation controlled bank note production, while every former republic could create deposit money. The cash shortages meant long delays in payments and an inevitable buildup in the magnitude of arrears.

Second, there was a breakdown in the payments system. As it was, the system was slow and payments, as noted earlier, took more than three to four weeks. Payments systems usually require arrangements between

---

[20]See Hardy and Lahiri (1994).

clearing, which involves the transmission of payment instructions, and settling, which involves the actual transfer of moneys to the intended beneficiary. Because settling the payments individually may take quite some time, clearing arrangements envisage a netting transaction under which each participant in the system must ensure maintenance of sufficient funds to cover its net balance to the system. In the Russian Federation, this proved to be difficult, as participants did not have sufficient reserves to maintain their net balance. In the circumstances, each successive payment is held owing to lack of payment by another participant.

The above discussion shows that, while sudden changes in policies may have unintended effects, the effects may be compounded by the lack of an efficient payments system. This, in turn, illustrates the crucial nature of the payments system. Although the improvements to these systems may not have prevented the occurrence of interenterprise arrears, they would have gone a long way toward reducing the magnitude of the problem.

2

Morphology of Government Accounting

Government accounting has traveled a long distance during the last two and a half millennia. Writing about government accounts, Kautilya noted, a long time ago, that their purpose was to keep precise and detailed accounts of the king's landed property, crops, cattle, and other assets and of revenue and expenditure. To serve these purposes, he classified the accounting heads, or chapters, as they have come to be known, under which transactions were to be recorded and how daily accounts were to be submitted on a monthly basis. His framework included the maintenance of accounts of transactions and a list of punishments for the "more than forty ways" of stealing government money.[1] Accounting constituted an integral part of the state craft. Since the unveiling of double-entry bookkeeping a little more than five hundred years ago, some governments have moved to this type of system, although many still maintain accounts on a single-entry basis.

Notwithstanding this long history of accounting, it is difficult to find another aspect of government that has been subjected to as much criticism. It would appear that the main function of government accounting was one of solid housekeeping, reviewing the legal aspects of payments made and, as discussed in the previous chapter, ensuring the safekeeping of moneys collected on behalf of the state. From this internal housekeeping function, it developed to a stage where accounts of transactions conducted in a fiscal year were submitted to the legislature for information and, over the years, for its scrutiny and approval. While the primary objectives are not disputed, serving these objectives and doing so effectively have become issues of concern and serious debate. While the debate reflects the public's growing awareness of a subject that was hitherto considered a part of the arcane world of government, it also shows that the

---

[1]See Kautilya (1992). The detailed enumeration of various steps to be taken in the maintenance and inspection of accounts suggests that the age of calculators had arrived a long time before the lamentation by Edmund Burke, *Reflections on the Revolution in France*, that "the age of chivalry is gone. That of Sophisters, Calculators and Economists has succeeded."

expectations of what accounting systems should do have risen. Popular thinking about government accounts suggests a "trust deficit": although the public cannot be viewed as homogeneous, it seems that a cross section of people hold the view that accounts conceal more than they reveal and are deliberately couched in language that impedes comprehension.

Some critics contend that over the years government accounting has lost sight of the user. Program managers in government spending agencies, for their part, emphasize that budgetary accounts are legally specified to be maintained for a still undefined "consumer" and are not designed in most cases to serve the interests of policy management. Economists engaged in analyzing the performance of government fiscal policies find many accounting procedures and concepts perplexing, generally out of date, and without solid anchors, and, as such, liable to easy manipulation.[2] Each of these segments of public opinion would appear to hold the view that the accounts may be useful to others (presumably as an extension of labor theory of value and benefit of doubt approach, that is, that what is produced should be of some value and should be used by someone).

Although these criticisms are by no means new, several developments have made government accounts and accounting systems more responsive to changing needs and thus more eclectic. First is the widely perceived institutional failure in governments to respond to the demands of macroeconomic management. Pursuit of fiscal policies, either in a market context, in the framework of a structural adjustment, or in countries in the throes of transition from a command to a market-oriented economy, requires a good deal of data to equip managers with a keen eye for anticipation, a capacity for scenario planning, and an ability to reach decisions quickly and, more important, to implement them with minimum delay. As an integral part of this experience, the public wants information, not merely on *how much* has been collected, spent, and borrowed, but on *how* the funds have been spent. Attention has shifted to the effectiveness of the services provided and to a search for answers to the perennial question of whether they could have been provided at a lower cost. These concerns have prompted a detailed consideration of existing accounting practices and available options for improvement.

---

[2]In the United States, the legislation relating to the Chief Financial Officers' Act of 1990 (Section 102 (a)) states that the accounts "do not accurately disclose the current and probable future costs of operating and investment decisions, including the future needs of cash or other resources, do not permit adequate comparison of actual costs among executive agencies, and do not provide the timely information required for efficient management of programs" (Joint Financial Management Improvement Program, 1992a).

Second, the old debate about the applicability of commercial accounting, which was somewhat theological in the early 1950s, has become more pragmatic. The focus during recent years has been on the modifications needed to apply commercial accounting practices to the unique requirements of a government. A good deal of progress has been made toward this end, lending validity to the popular dictum that it is more productive to engage in practical steps, however small, than to discuss abstracts ad infinitum.

Third, the revolution in computer technology has permitted the exploration of new areas. The relevant question is no longer whether it is possible to apply this technology to government accounting but how it can be applied. Because of these developments, what can be done in accounting is limited not by innovative capability but by technology. Thus, government accounting is at the threshold of major change. This and the following chapters provide background for these changes and discuss their impact on the current and future shape of government accounting.

Commercial and Government Accounting

For several decades, the debate in governmental circles centered on the applicability of commercial accounting formats to the operations of public authorities. It has been argued that commercial accounting, which has been expressed in abstract and general terms, was not applicable to governments, whose operations were directed toward providing goods and services and not toward making profits. The argument was dogmatic and oversimplified the issues. Even as this debate was being conducted in public, the governments of several countries had introduced double-entry bookkeeping and annual balance sheets by the early 1950s. In governments that, in principle, had single-entry bookkeeping and were thus considered uniquely distinguishable from the commercial world, there were pro forma balance sheets and double-entry bookkeeping for what were considered to be commercial activities. For example, in British India, Irrigation (commercial) was distinguished from Irrigation (noncommercial), and the former had different accounting systems that were drawn partly from commercial accounting practices.

In the centrally planned economies, accounting both in government and in publicly owned enterprises (although the techniques took a wide variety of forms) had three functions. The first function was to maintain financial records of revenues, expenses, assets, and liabilities. The second was to maintain an elaborate system (some suggest too elaborate, lending itself to manipulation and imaginative construction of data) for recording and maintaining aggregate economic data, including volume of production, costs of production, productivity, and installed capacity. Third, in purely commercial or manufacturing industries, additional record keeping was organized to monitor the stocks of materials and products. Thus, the debate was essentially restricted to the British-type systems, which traditionally used single-entry bookkeeping systems. The argument emphasized that the purposes of accounting in government were to assist the budgetary allocation of funds and related financial management of flows. As a corollary, it was pointed out that the source of funds is not directly related to the provision of goods and services: funds are drawn from the proceeds of general taxation, while the provision of goods and services has its own political and financial rationale and in any event does not entirely hinge on the recovery of costs through a user charge and associated methods of pricing. Further, there was no open market mechanism to determine the demand for government services.

These features may be unique to a government but do not necessarily call for a different accounting system as long as the system entails recording, analyzing, classifying, and interpreting financial information relating to government transactions. It is now widely accepted that any accounting system in the government, as in any organization regardless of its commercial orientation, should facilitate the recognition of financial management performance, show the progress made by each agency in achieving its objectives, and highlight areas that require further oversight. Consequently, some elements of commercial accounting have gained gradual acceptance in government circles. A number of concrete events have contributed to the change in attitude that permitted this transformation of government accounting.

First, over the years, the size and complexity of government operations have increased as the government has become engaged in procuring complex machinery and using it for a variety of purposes. This development created the need for a system that would facilitate the maintenance of records of assets as well as data for the computation of fixed and variable costs. Second, economic management has begun to make more demands on the type and timely supply of accounting information. In particular, changes in the domestic economy, such as inflation, hyperinflation, or recession, require adjustments in historical data for analytical purposes.

Third, accounting data became necessary to measure the performance of organizations so as to serve the immediate purpose of policy formulation and the broader purpose of accountability. Accountability has evolved from being limited to the observance of laws and regulations on the flow of resources to being concerned with the uses of allotted resources and the effectiveness with which those resources are used. Fourth, accounting has to address not only immediate liabilities but also those that would be redeemed at a later stage. It became imperative to strengthen accounting systems so that they would be able to measure and disclose these liabilities.

Fifth, the role of external aid and related conditionality required the adoption of internationally accepted government standards for maintenance of accounts. As most of the aid was used for specific commercial or quasi-commercial purposes, it required the introduction of the commercial type of accounting in those areas of government that were funded by foreign aid. Similar insistence on standards by regional organizations, such as the European Union, also contributed to major changes in the accounting practices of member countries as well as those aspiring to become members.

Finally, the extended application of computer technology to the processing of financial information and associated benefits effectively put an end to the debate about the chasm between government and the private sector and the inapplicability of commercial accounting practices to public sector transactions. Although government is different from other entities, standards can be devised to reflect the different approaches and practices of government.

Accounting systems in government are generally divided into four categories, which in turn reveal the nature of the organization and its activities: (1) fund accounting for governmental organizations, such as ministries, departments, bureaus, and agencies, that are primarily engaged in formulating and implementing policies; (2) quasi-fund accounting systems of agencies that are engaged in regulatory and related activities, including the oversight of organizations that provide services. In their orientation, these agencies are not distinguishable from departments and ministries but are usually given an autonomous status, including separate budgets largely funded by the government; (3) quasi-commercial systems dealing with public utilities that function, for all intents and purposes, like commercial organizations but that are obliged to pursue noncommercial objectives specified by the government; and (4) commercial accounting systems in organizations and agencies or enterprises that are largely owned and controlled by the government and that pursue their activities on a commercial basis. Of these four activities, however, the third and fourth would be viewed as belonging to the commercial world and are thus obliged to have commercial accounting systems. The first two categories are relevant to this discussion.

Three accounting bases are recognized for the organizations specified in categories 1 and 2, namely, accrual basis, cash basis, and budgetary accounting. The first two categories are discussed in detail below. Budgetary accounting is used to track the different stages of budget implementation and comes into action after a budget has been approved for the fiscal year. It addresses the implementation of the budget after the requisite legal authority, which differs from one country to another, becomes available. Although the details of budget accounting differ from system to system, the common stages usually include *appropriation* (a legal authority specifying the amounts available for spending during the fiscal year), *apportionment* (a time-sliced release of budgetary authority that may take the form of a warrant), *obligation* (a firm order for the purchase of goods and services invoiced either immediately before or after the transaction or at a specified later date), *actual payment*, and *delivery* of goods and services. The emphasis of the system, which is common to all organizations regardless of their ownership, is to show the extent to which appropriations have been encumbered and have been paid.

Single- and Double-Entry Bookkeeping

One of the main distinctions between government[3] and commercial accounting is the way in which accounts are maintained. Most transactions in governments are maintained on a single-entry basis.[4] Single-entry bookkeeping, which is generally defined in negative terms as the one that is not double-entry bookkeeping, refers to a system of record keeping in which transactions are noted in a single record, such as a checkbook, a cashbook, or a vote book. Although subsidiary records may be maintained to register commitments made and goods and services received, the focus of the system is on the single record. Thus, a spending agency engaged in normal policy formulation and related administration may maintain a single book showing the payments it has made. Such a system has been and continues to be in operation in several countries, largely because most departments do not have an independent source of funding and depend on budgetary appropriations to finance their activities. Ac-

---

[3]The term "government" is used here rather generally. As will be noted from the discussion in this section, there may be areas where double-entry bookkeeping may be in practice in some parts of the government. The reference here is to the predominant practice.

[4]This discussion is largely relevant to the British Commonwealth countries. Countries that follow the French, Latin American, or American-type systems usually have a double-entry bookkeeping approach.

cordingly, they maintain a single record that records the outflows. Revenues collected by the agency usually form part of a general pool known as the general account or consolidated funds of the government. The system was designed to be simple in a context where payments were handled in the various corners of a country by entry-level staff with little or no professional training or experience in accounting. Their principal function was to make entries in the chronological sequence in which they occurred, which were then sifted and consolidated into a government account. At a consolidated level, the outflows matched the inflows.

In double-entry bookkeeping, each transaction is recorded as a credit and a debit entry. It records what flows in and what flows out. But such recording takes place at two levels—a journal and a ledger. A journal is a first level of record keeping that registers the transactions as they take place. Such recording is called an entry, and these accounts are viewed as nominal accounts. These are then included in a ledger (the transfer from the journal is called "posting," and the accounts are viewed as real to distinguish them from the nominal journal-level accounts). The ledger accounts are more analytical and specify amounts to be received, amounts to be paid, assets acquired, and changes in cash balances, thus showing the assets and liabilities that constitute a part of a balance sheet. The journal is a preparatory stage for the ledger, which takes into account the two aspects of the transactions. Unlike the single-entry system, the double-entry system is complete and fully reflects the financial status of the entity.

In considering whether double-entry bookkeeping can be extended to government accounting three issues need to be addressed. Is this type of bookkeeping necessary? Is it viable? Is it economical? Although these three are not mutually exclusive, they offer different analytical points of departure for the debate.

As noted above, the strongest argument in favor of a single-entry system is the long tradition of spending ministries' having no source of revenue and of not being expected, at least in the view of those who favor strong centralized financial management, to serve as repositories of financial responsibility. Such approaches are not in accord with the trends that favor endowing the agencies with more financial responsibility. Once the agencies are given the task of self-accounting, they must have adequate accounting standards. This in turn implies a system of recording transactions at two stages, that is, journals and ledgers. The agencies need systems that measure their financial resources and, more important from the point of view of stable management, a record of funded and unfunded liabilities. Thus, the conversion from single- to double-entry bookkeeping is an imperative of the times.

Does the introduction of double-entry bookkeeping contribute to any major dislocation in work and is it viable in the long term? Again, as noted previously, double-entry bookkeeping is already in practice in public organizations, and extending it to the rest of the government is not problematic. Indeed, in some countries, for example, Chile, such an extension has reduced the perceived differences between commercial and government accounting practices. Accounting as taught in the universities equips graduates to move in both worlds and to move from one to the other with ease. Although accounting standards—that is, the treatment of specific items in the balance sheet—in the commercial world and in government may differ, newly trained accountants would be equally familiar with the two approaches. The availability of a pool of human resources with uniform training contributes additional strength to the operation of a system.

The general ledger system described further on may also prove economical because it is operated on the computer and is based on double-entry accounting. It thus requires fewer resources than the traditional system, which was manually operated and tended to be more expensive. Switching from one system to the other will contribute to improved financial management and is also likely to be less expensive over the long term and to offer enhanced, multifaceted capacity.

Cash and Accrual

The bases of budgeting and terms of accounting are primarily considered in terms of cash, accrual, and obligations. Although in some cases the obligational basis is also considered a kind of accrual, it is different. The choice of the basis was governed more by tradition than by rational and calculated review. Basically, budget systems are viewed as either budget funding or budget limiting. The former is intended to provide a greater role for the legislature, which, after due consideration, appropriates or funds a program or project for its entire life. Such appropriations have their own life cycles and are not limited to a fiscal year. As a matter of common practice, these funds, once appropriated, have an average life of more than four to five years and may be extended until, in due course, they become regular components of the annual budget. This system, also known as obligations-based, allows the legislature to look into the continuing relevance of a project or a program and to determine its future.

The budget-limiting system, in contrast, focuses on the amounts to be spent or the limits beyond which spending is not to be undertaken during a fiscal year. The intent is to recognize the paramount role of the legislature in making the annual budget and endowing it with the requisite flexibility. At the time these systems evolved, little weight was attached to the monetary implications of the budget. Within this overall framework, some countries followed an accounting system that bore close resemblance to the commercial accounting system in that they used a double-entry bookkeeping procedure and balance sheets that included, among other items, the liabilities and assets of the entity. These practices, however, were relegated to the background in the early 1970s, when emphasis was laid on the pursuit of macroeconomic policies aimed at economic stabilization. As an integral part of this emphasis, cash-based systems, which are inherently better for reconciling monetary data and for measuring more precisely the impact of budgetary operations on the credit situation specifically and on the economy in general, gained acceptance.

Some Western industrial democracies switched to a cash-based system from an obligations- or accrual-based system. After about two decades of experience with cash-based systems, however, there has been a revival of demand for the restoration of accrual-based systems, and a few countries in the South Pacific have already begun to transform the traditional system into an accrual-based one. These efforts, it should be noted, are being made in those countries that originally followed the budget-limiting approach. Countries using obligations- and funding-based systems may also need to reorient their accounting systems. Because the demand for accrual accounting is likely to increase in the future, it is appropriate to consider the features of these systems, the arguments in favor of cash and accrual systems (and the related issue of whether the choice between the two is real), the relationships between budget and accounts, and the implementation aspects of the switch to an accrual system.

Terms and Definitions

The terminology, such as obligations, commitments, cash-based system, and accrual, both in the literature and in general practice, has not been free from ambiguity. To define the terms, it is necessary to recapitulate briefly the various steps in the budget process. When an entity is authorized to incur an obligation—that is, to enter into a contractual type of transaction in which an order is placed—then the budget system is *obligations-based*. When the budget is based on the amounts likely to be disbursed, it is considered *cash-based*. Once the budget is approved, it is implemented through a series of steps: *apportionment; internal allotment*—a method for dividing the aggregate amounts within an agency to various claimants, such as divisions in the entity or programs; *obligation*—placement of an order (in some cases a further distinction is made between an obligation and a commitment, the latter being a firm and irrevocable order); *disbursement* to record the payment; and the *expense*, where the actual use of the materials acquired is recorded. All accounting systems, regardless of origin and current orientation, are expected, in principle, to record these various stages, although noncompliance is common. While capturing these stages, however, the accounting system may have a primary orientation that is based on cash or on accrual.

In a cash-based accounting system, revenues and expenditures are recorded only when cash is received or paid out. The system does not take into account the period to which transactions apply. A cash-based system may also include noncash transactions, such as foreign aid received in kind, or the book adjustments made among government agencies when the products of one are delivered to another. A few countries operate what is usually known as a modified cash basis, which includes payments made in a particular period for transactions that were budgeted in a previous year.

Accrual accounting refers to the acquisition of goods and services regardless of payments received or paid out. This conventional definition has been further expanded by the U.S. Federal Accounting Standards Advisory Board[5] to include transactions, events, and circumstances that have a financial effect regardless of when cash is paid out or received. This enlarged definition seeks to go beyond the goods and services to policy decisions regarding transfers (pensions and other welfare payments, which have tended to dominate the budgets of several countries) so that all types of liabilities can be captured. Some countries use a modified accrual basis, which involves essentially cash-based accounts adjusted to reflect an accrual basis. Both the modified cash and the accrual basis exemplify systemic responses to policymakers' periodic demands for additional information; the accounting standards of these systems are not consistent over time, however.

Why Accrual Now?

Cash accounting facilitates the regular assessment of the impact of fiscal activity on the economy and contributes to a reconciliation of the monetary data, which is handled on a cash basis. However, a cash system is in-

---

[5]See its Exposure Draft (1991).

effective in indicating the immediate, medium-term, and long-term liabilities of a government. For example, the pension liabilities of a government are generally understated, and, more often than not, the budgetary outcome is higher than the estimates included in the budget. Moreover, in cash-based accounting, transactions are recorded as payments are made, and a more detailed inquiry is needed to determine whether the payment is for services rendered during the current or the previous year. Matching payments to income and cost of services in a specific time frame (fiscal year) is rendered difficult. Inasmuch as the information about liabilities is not fully captured, it has been argued that cash-based accounting may unwittingly contribute to distorted fiscal decision making, and legislatures may be called upon to provide a pro forma approval for spending obligations that have already been incurred.

The merits of the accrual system also need to be recognized.[6] In contrast to the cash-based system, the accrual-based system seeks to provide a comprehensive picture of all government liabilities, thereby aiding the formulation of realistic fiscal policies. It also facilitates orderly cash management through its explicit portrayal of liabilities. More specifically, it helps fiscal policymakers see beyond the current fiscal year and the next year's budget. During periods of acute fiscal crisis, the accrual-based system allows policymakers to see beyond the transactions of the week or the month to the medium term and, in particular, to focus on the contingent liabilities and hidden liabilities looming large on the horizon.

At a program management level, accrual-based accounting provides an accurate picture of the full costs by capturing, in addition to cash flows, overhead costs, including the value of the physical assets used in the provision of services. Similarly, estimates of full resource costs, in addition to helping the budgetary allocation of resources, would also facilitate decision making in determining which services the government should provide and which should be contracted out to private suppliers.

The debate during recent years has tended to focus on the relative merits of one form of accounting over another. A more important question is: Why choose between the two systems? In reality, the relationship between the two is a symbiotic one and the two cannot be considered separately. The cash system is less complex and easier to administer, and years of tradition have made it a first choice. It is also true that it has several blind spots and can no longer fully serve the complex demands of public policymakers. It needs to be supplemented by accrual-based accounting so as

---

[6]For a more recent statement, see Organization for Economic Cooperation and Development (1993).

to provide a fuller picture of the liabilities and costs of operations. When payments are recorded in a cash system, it is assumed that goods and services have been delivered and that the associated liabilities are being liquidated. Conversely, an accrual system assumes that when liabilities are recorded, arrangements are being made to finance them. Together, the two systems provide full information, and the expenditure manager will be better served by drawing on elements of each. Fortunately, modern computer technology permits the recording of each stage of a transaction. Supplementary systems can then be developed for the preparation of the balance sheets and full cost information.

Budget and Accounts

In governments, the coverage, basis, and classification of budgets and accounts are closely linked. Essentially, the accounting system follows the parameters of the budget and provides the needed information at the various stages of budget formulation and implementation. To the extent, however, that the accounting system is accrual-based, the data it reports would differ materially from data used to formulate and implement a budget that is not based on accrual. The significant issue is whether the budget should also be placed on an accrual basis.

The experiences of a few countries, such as Australia, Iceland, and New Zealand, show a diversity of approaches to budgeting and accounting. With the gradual development of accounting standards and extended application of accrual-based accounting systems, it is likely that the debate over the merits of the different accounting systems will lead to convergent approaches. Meanwhile, it is appropriate to consider the various aspects of this issue. As a preliminary step, the following continuum in government financial management comprising the budgeting, accounting, and reporting systems needs to be noted:

Budget appropriation	→	Accrued expenditures	→	Cash payments	→	Reporting on performance and fiscal developments

Any system adopted should reflect the budget concerns, entry into and liquidation of claims, and reporting on performance. It has been argued that the budget system should continue to be primarily a cash-based one for three reasons. First, the budget, as an economic document, should indicate the likely monetary impact of government operations on the economy. From this point of view, the cash-based budget offers an advantage. Second, most of the legislative ceilings and related limits are specified in cash terms and to that extent a cash-based budget would be appropriate. Third, most control operations in government are anchored in a cash basis, and the approaches to cash management, which have a crucial role to play in heavily indebted economies, would be better served by cash systems.

These arguments tend to ignore the foundation of accrual accounting that has been accepted, as discussed earlier, primarily for two reasons. First, legislative authorities as well as policymakers in the executive branch of government should have information on the full cost of programs and projects, and, second, effective planning and financial management in the spending agencies require accrual-based accounting systems.

Each system has certain strengths and, as argued earlier, attempts to choose between the two and to consider each one to the exclusion of the other contribute to an avoidable controversy. In Australia, accrual budgeting has been introduced as an adjunct to cash budgeting. In Iceland, the decision has been to present the budget to the legislature on both an accrual and a cash basis. Data presented for each department distinguish between cash receipts and expenditures and accrued receipts and expenditures. In New Zealand, government activities have been divided into three categories: purchasing outputs (Mode A), functioning primarily as an owner (Mode B), and providing benefits (Mode C). For Mode A, which focuses only on inputs, appropriations are made on a cash basis. In Mode B, attention shifts to the consumption of resources and may operate on a "net" or a "gross" basis. Capital injections and related budgetary provisions are made on a cash basis but are expected to be fully supported by adequate documentation on the full cost of producing output.

For those activities that revolve around the administration of transfer payments, appropriations are made on a cash basis. In all these cases, however, the budget documents have been strengthened to include operating statements and statements of projected performance. From 1994, appropriations are made in both cash and accrual terms, and, in addition, ample financial information is provided on an accrual basis. In the United States, the legislature will continue to approve the annual budget on a cash basis (within the overall framework of program obligations) although accounting statements would be on accrual basis. These different approaches should not add materially to the work burden and, in any event, any costs would be offset by the benefits that are expected to accrue.

Dimensions of the Issue

How does the introduction of accrual accounting in government affect the presentation of the budget? While the answer is dependent on the legislative tradition and the basis of appropriation, from a technical point of view, it depends on the items included in the budget and the way they are treated in cash- and accrual-based budgets and accounts. For this purpose, the treatment of the main components of object-wise classification, which is common to all the agencies in the government, is illustrated in Table 7.

Substantive differences exist in payments for goods and services and for capital expenditures. In these cases, the cash basis offers an inadequate picture of the actual extent to which liabilities have been incurred and could thus contribute to misleading conclusions about the real state of finances. The accrual-based system has an advantage in that it illustrates the full extent of the resources needed to finance decisions already made by the government. The establishment of accrual-based budgets, where cash-based accounting is in use, should start from the bottom: each agency's estimates should be expressed in both cash and accrual terms, with an explanation of the differences. Such a presentation would serve the informational needs of legislators, policymakers, effective internal financial management, and cash management for the whole government. The application of computer technology makes this task somewhat simpler than might appear at first sight.

General Ledger System

At the core of government financial management (which is now considered under various names, such as Integrated Financial Management Systems (IFMS) and Integrated Functional Budget and Accounting Systems (IFBAS)) is the general ledger, in which all inflows and outflows are finally recorded. The role of the ledger in the budget system is to track the status of appropriations, indicating amounts committed and the linkages between commitments and payments (Diagram 1). The ledger also plays a role in treasury operations, serving as the channel through which most transactions are carried out.

This core (general ledger) is then linked to the subsidiary systems that must be maintained by either the central or spending agencies. An illustration of this is provided in Diagram 2. In a more simplified form, when the budget is organized in the traditional line-item format, the agencies

Diagram 1. Core Application

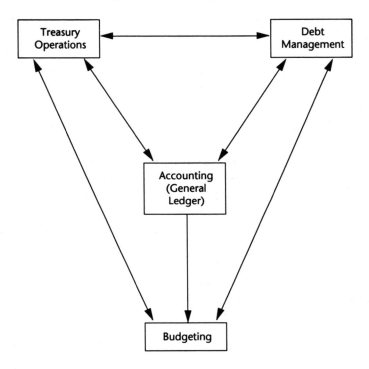

may be required, in pursuance of the traditional orientation and methods of control, to maintain commitment control entries, funds distribution among various entities, and applications for virements or reappropriation from one accounting head to another. In addition, each agency, depending on its main activity, may be required to maintain special computer files for travel, utility payments, pensions, inventory management, foreign aid, revenue refunds, and assets disposed of in the context of privatization. The range of files that could be opened is fairly large and is limited only by the capacity of hardware and software and by the technological status of the communications system.

Notwithstanding the obvious appeal of the computer-operated general ledger system (whether based on customized software or off-the-shelf software—of which several packages are available and more are likely to become available with the increasing acceptance of this approach and consequent expansion of the market), several issues have been raised about the way in which the system should be implemented and the preparatory steps that need to be taken. At this stage, it is premature to discuss various points: whether the introduction should be through a

Table 7. Cash- and Accrual-Based Budgets

Category	Cash-Based Budget	Accrual-Based Budget	Remarks
Current expenditures			
Personal emoluments and related benefits	Budget estimates would be based on the cash amounts likely to be paid during the year.	Estimates would reflect the complete liability.	Differences between the two would be minimal in most cases. In some cases, actual cash payments may be lower than the accrual-based estimates when, for example, a new pay revision is approved but payments may not be made in full and may be spread over more than one fiscal year.
Purchases of goods and services	As above, estimates reflect the likely actual disbursement during the year.	Estimates would be based on orders placed regardless of delivery or their payment or the actual use of the goods and services received.	Differences arise in the following cases: (1) When substantial lags exist in the delivery of goods and services, cash estimates would be different. (2) When payments are likely to be carried over as a part of a policy of "liability management," cash estimates would be lower. (3) Cash outlays could be higher when substantial arrears carried over from previous years are proposed to be fully paid.
Debt service	In principle, cash estimates are based on accrual method, in that repayments due and the interest payable on outstanding debt are taken into account.	Estimates are based on the levels of outstanding debt and related repayments and interest costs. Future debt estimates are based on forecasts.	Actual cash outlays could be less when a part of the debt is capitalized and carried forward. But, in general, the differences between the two would be minimal.
Pensions and entitlements	Estimates would be based on the likely magnitudes of payments.	Estimates would be based on the liabilities specified in the relevant legislation. Although the liabilities could be open ended, the annual estimates would be limited to the liabilities estimated to be liquidated during the year.	Differences arise in the following cases: (1) When pensions are organized on a separate basis outside the regular budget, the transfers made from the budget may be less than actually indicated. (2) In cases of acute stringency, some payments may be held over and carried forward to the next year.

Subsidies and grants to public enterprises	Estimates would be based on the relevant legislation and price forecasts.	Basis is the same as in cash estimates.	Differences may arise only insofar as it is determined that the actual payments should be less than the liabilities indicated by legislation and price forecasts.
Grants to other levels of government and nongovernmental organizations	Based on relevant legislation.	Based on relevant legislation.	As above.
Capital expenditures			
Material assets	Based on the estimated payments regardless of actual liabilities.	Based on estimated contractual liabilities and actual progress of physical work.	Differences could be considerable, and much would depend on the cash payment schedules that may be formulated independent of the physical aspects. The differences could be substantial in regard to donor-financed equipment. Further, year-end balance sheets could reflect the market rather than the acquisition value.
Financial investments	Based on policy decisions to acquire financial assets and to make other investments.	As in the case of cash-based estimates.	Differences arise in balance sheet presentation in that the investments would be shown at market value rather than at acquired value.
Lending	As above.	As above	Differences arise annually when the loan portfolio is assessed and nonperforming loans are written off.

Diagram 2. Overall Financial Management System

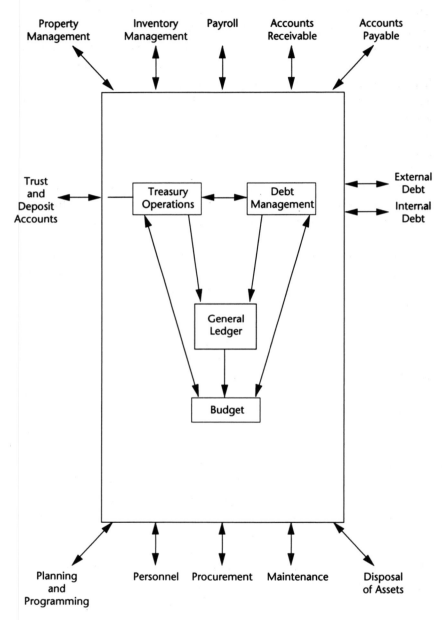

Illustrates the interaction between core and specialized information systems. The specialized systems shown here are illustrative and not exhaustive.

mainframe or through a linkage among available personal computers; whether separate arrangements should be made to hire space in the satellite so that information could be collected from the regions; and whether an earth station is needed and, if so, the financial implications of such arrangements. Technology is changing rapidly. It is also becoming fiercely competitive, so that estimates of financial implications, which differ from country to country in any case, change rapidly as well. The only assertion that can be made about the future is that a financial manager will have more technological choices and less expensive arrangements than in the past.

Two issues arise in the preparation of the existing systems to facilitate the application of the general ledger system. They are the fund structure and the traditional budget classification. Fund systems in government are generally categorized as limited, intermediate, or extensive. When channeled through five or fewer funds, the system is considered limited. Systems with 5–20 funds are regarded as intermediate, and those with more funds are viewed as extensive. These limits are drawn for purely analytical purposes, and the conventional belief is that as the number of funds grows, transactions among them grow exponentially and may contribute to a loss of control. In addition, more personnel may be required to manage the funds. In the context of a computer-operated general ledger, the number of funds does not pose a major problem. Each fund will be recognized as a subsidiary or as a special system with regular, specific linkages to the general ledger (Diagram 2). Similarly, the nomenclature of the budget does not pose a problem, as the entries in the ledger will reflect the categories of the budget. However, it would be incongruous to apply advanced technology to a conventional approach to control. Rather, the potential of the technology should be used to effect a substantive change in the approaches to budgetary control. Experience has shown conclusively that when essential changes are not made in the budget categories and related controls, computer processing ends up as a quick mechanical adjunct to the conventional process.

A related issue is the impact of technology on the control exercised by the central agencies. Hitherto, the centralized system of control was based on two premises: (1) the finance ministry should exercise the control, and (2) most control should be exercised through the traditional verification methods, at the payment stage. Although valid in an earlier time, these premises are open to criticism in a context where modern technology has made instant information possible, thereby leveling the playing field. The role of the finance ministry is now to monitor developments once a budget is approved and to provide guidance to the spending agencies on cost-effective methods of resource utilization. The general ledger system thus serves as a clearinghouse for recent developments and makes it easier for participants to anticipate likely trends. Decision makers who once relied on their proverbial sixth sense to anticipate situations can now rely on the general ledger for the identification of vulnerable areas. Under this system, control is more meaningful and therefore more effective.

The implementation of the general ledger system offers, in theory, a choice—a massive overnight shift or the more evolutionary approach of spreading through pilot projects and learning from experience at each stage. In practice, however, the choice has been limited to the evolutionary approach. Experience shows that limiting initial projects to headquarters and the major spending agencies is appropriate. Later, the projects can be extended to the regions and field operations.

Government Accounts and National Income Accounts

In the commercial world, the annual balance sheet and related statements on income and expenditure and sources and uses of funds make the accumulation accounts and the flows during the year for which these statements relate more transparent. A counterpart of this in the government sector is the national income accounts (NIA), which are primarily based on accounting data and seek to compare and aggregate heterogeneous information from the government accounts to compile comparable data in this subsector over time. These accounts thus provide data on current revenue, current expenditure or consumption, net saving, and gross capital formation and how it has been financed. The accounts answer questions that arise in the formulation of the annual budget about the optimum level of public accumulation and annual capital investment. Although decisions continue to be more political than economic in their orientation (and in developing countries, this responsibility is often shared with donor governments and international and regional financial institutions), the NIA provide an empirical basis for such decisions. The NIA, as policy accounts, are different from the government's closed accounts, which, in most cases, must be audited, submitted to the legislature, or published.

The NIA have several subaccounts that relate to the general government (central government plus local governments); public sector (general government plus state-owned enterprises); state enterprise operations; tax statistics; transfer expenditures including interest, subsidies, and other transfers; outlays on the environment; expenditure on social welfare; and outlays of the main departments, such as defense. These subaccounts are detailed to facilitate the netting of transactions to arrive at analytically meaningful subaggregates. For policy purposes, the NIA may also be supplemented by generational accounts (see discussion below). Both NIA and generational accounts represent separate analytical constructions, based mostly on government accounts but partly on separate supplementary investigations to enable policymakers to ascertain the current status of government finances and to make decisions thereon.

Government accounts also shed light on the status of government finances but in a more technical and somewhat narrower way. They represent the first stage from which the NIA are drawn. Until recently, government accounts did not provide accumulation accounts (that is, an accumulation of assets and liabilities); nor did they separate, as in the commercial world, operational budgets from investment budgets. If, however, the complete commercial formats of accounting are applied to public entities, the compilation of such accounts would be rendered easy. Meanwhile, the NIA seek to provide this information. In their present form and as applied across industrial and developing countries, the NIA are based on the methodology developed by the United Nations over two decades ago. This methodology has recently been refined further, and the NIA will, in the future, be based on the refined methodology.[7]

The NIA provide for both a current and a capital account to classify government transactions. While definitional approaches and related practices are, for the most part, congruent insofar as current consumption is concerned, they differ from prevailing practices with respect to the capital account. This is primarily because the capital budgets (and hence accounts) in governments reflect a wide variety of practices, indeed a veritable salmagundi, that are often different from the approaches indicated in the NIA. For example, expenditures on software and leasing of equipment are recorded in most budgets as current, while they would be shown in the NIA under the capital account. Similarly, outlays on the maintenance of a capital asset during the first year of its operation are conventionally recorded under capital expenditures in government budgets and accounts. There are several other details where the respective treatments differ, and these are illustrated in Table 8. A major issue relates to depreciation or estimates of consumption of fixed capital. These estimates require that regular data about the life of an asset as well as average prices for the period be maintained. Governments do not generally maintain depreciation accounts, and even when they do, the budgetary provisions

---

[7]See European Union and others (1993).

Table 8. Budgets, Accounts, and National Income Accounts

Description	Budget Systems	Accounting Systems	National Accounts
Coverage of the system	The coverage of the budget is, in principle, expected to be coterminous with that of the government. In practice, however, several transactions may be outside the budget.	Generally follow the purview of the budget. In some cases, extra-budgetary accounts may also be available on a consolidated basis.	Coverage is complete and includes all transactions, whether organized as a part of the budget or outside, of the central and general governments.
Current and capital distinctions	Very few governments have current and capital budgets. Several practices represent variations of this theme.	Broadly follow the budget systems. In some cases, governments are now required to prepare annual balance sheets showing both stocks and flows.	Require both accumulation accounts and balance sheets. These accounts are drawn from the regular accounts of a government. If these data are not adequate, subsidiary systems are established to collect the needed data.
Scope of capital account	In general, those items that have prospective benefits, a life span of more than one year, are above a specified monetary ceiling, and usually financed by debt are included in the capital budget.	Follow the budgetary practice.	Cover assets that are owned (and therefore can be disposed of) by governments and those that have prospective economic benefits.
Acquisition of existing assets			
Flows during the year	Recorded at the purchase value of the asset. If they are acquired over a period of years, each year's budget shows only a part of the total outlay.	Broadly follow the budgetary practice. For purposes of balance sheets, the concept of constructive delivery may be used, and parts of assets would be deemed to have been acquired. But few governments are currently preparing consolidated annual balance sheets.	Recorded in the system, and, where progress payments are made, the concept of constructive delivery is invoked.

Stocks	Stocks of assets are not recorded in the budget or its associated documents.	Stocks of assets must be shown where the governments maintain balance sheets on commercial lines. Mostly, however, this information is not available.	Information on the accumulated levels is systematically included.
Assets built during the year	Outlays incurred during the year are shown. Total outlay on an asset is generally not shown. Also, the concept of constructive delivery is not applied.	Reflects the situation as in the budget. Concept of constructive delivery is generally not applied.	Fully recorded and imputations are made for work in progress with reference to the concept of constructive delivery.
Financial assets Loans[1]	Only the flows (and not the stocks) are shown in the budget.	Accounts show mostly flows.	Now required to be compiled on a comprehensive basis for the accumulation accounts and balance sheets.
Shares and investment	As above.	As above.	
Monetary gold, SDR allocations, and related investments	Generally not included in the budget of the government.	These and the stocks in regard to the above items are mostly shown in the balance sheets of the central bank.	
Capital transfers	Shown in the budget; data are limited to flows. However, the end use of these transfers could be and often is different from the intent.		Required to be recorded on a comprehensive basis. For end use, the approaches indicated in the Frascati Manual may be utilized. In addition, debt cancellation by mutual agreement is recorded as a capital transfer (this information is generally not available in the budget).
Capital assets	Only amounts spent during the year on the acquisition or life renewal of these assets are shown in the budget.	Data mostly restricted to flows.	

Table 8 (*concluded*)

Description	Budget Systems	Accounting Systems	National Accounts
Cultivated assets	Outlays on computer software and others are usually considered as consumption expenditures.	Most government accounts show only those transactions recorded in the budget. Where, however, supplementary balance sheets are prepared, value of commercial forests, national parks, etc. is shown. Plantations and orchards may be shown only when they are extensive or are on a commercial scale.	Required to be included in the national accounts.
Intangible assets		These are generally recorded only where balance sheet approach is used. Even then, they would be recognized only when a foreseeable future benefit is perceived.	Explicitly recognized in the national accounts.
Assets acquired through barter and foreign aid	Barter transactions are not usually recorded in the budget. Assets acquired through foreign aid are generally shown, although there are enormous data gaps.	Barter transactions may not be recognized. Assets acquired through foreign aid are recorded.	All assets, including those acquired through barter, are required to be included in the national accounts.
Treatment of selected items			
Valuation	Outlays reflect the acquisition value. Stocks, as noted above, are not shown.	Stocks are mostly shown at acquired value; when commercial accounts are compiled, stocks are shown at the net current value.	All assets are required to be shown at their current market value.

Changes in inventories	Not normally recorded.	Included in systems that produce annual balance sheets.	Required to be included.
Depreciation	Included in few countries.	Included in few countries. Different classes of assets have specific lives.	Included in the national accounts.
Small tools	Mostly shown in the current or operational budget.	As in the budget system.	Treated as fixed assets when they form a significant part of the value of the total stock.
Military equipment	Outlays, except those on structures and dwellings, are considered as consumption expenditures.	As in the budget system.	Only structures and dwellings are considered as fixed assets.

[1]Amounts forgone, formally written off, or postponed may not be fully reflected either in the budget or in associated accounts.

tend to be arbitrary, more for the sake of form, and their utility for financial management is rendered moot. In this area, accounting standards that lend themselves to consistent and uniform application throughout the government need to be developed.

Several industrial countries have set up computerized, integrated data bases for all public accounts. Such data bases have become essential in view of the variety of demands made by economists, political authorities, and international institutions for fundamental statistical documentation at a detailed level. This, in turn, involves the compilation and maintenance of detailed building blocks on government transactions that can then be arranged and rearranged according to the user's requirements. These blocks are entirely menu-driven but in each case require the maintenance of a detailed data base. The introduction of commercial accounts, with a specific distinction between operational and investment budgets, and the related maintenance of detailed data bases would also facilitate the compilation of national income accounts.

Generational Accounts

It is now generally accepted that fiscal issues cannot be solved during one fiscal year and require concerted and consistent efforts over time to address them. This approach recognizes that most fiscal policymaking addresses the short-term concerns that may leave a lot, at any rate more than intended, to future generations—a long legacy of problems and fewer resources. Although policymakers do not resort to the philosophical predictions of religious leaders about the arrival of a savior, they tend to be optimistic about the future. This has several practical implications. Two cardinal principles of modern accounting are that there should be a match between resources and uses of funds in a time frame and that there should be intergenerational equity. The former principle requires that resources raised in a period should be adequate for the services provided and, as a corollary, that the citizens of the current period should not be shifting a part of the burden for payment to the next generation. However, the bulk of the expenditures incurred now on retirement, health care, and life insurance tend to understate current expenditures by shifting them to the future. Similarly, experience shows conclusively that during periods of fiscal stress, expenditures on routine repairs, maintenance, and replacement of assets are deferred to the point that their real value is substantially eroded by the time they are available to future generations. How should the accounting system reflect these realities and are its methods adequate?

Policymakers, including accountants and economists, recognize that measurement of economic performance over time is not merely important but essential. While economists tend to emphasize intergenerational equity, accountants have been trying to evolve methods, such as accrual, that illumine the assets and liabilities of public entities at any given time. But economists have developed another method to measure fiscal performance properly in the belief that existing methods are inadequate and that the deficit, as calculated, is "a number in search of a concept."[8] In the United States, economists have proposed that the Government replace the existing annual budget with a system of "generational accounts." Although such a major change is unlikely—largely because the system is now being reoriented after a long period of contemplation, analysis, and inaction—generational accounts are being used as an analytical device to illustrate the underlying trends in government finances.[9] Similar efforts are under way in Italy, Japan, and Norway, although in Italy the effort is restricted to an analytical study undertaken by the central bank and has not made any forays into the actual budgetary process. What then is the method of generational accounting? What are its strengths and vulnerabilities? Can it replace the existing budget system? Does it represent a major advance over the accrual accounting approach? These questions are considered below.

Generational accounting represents an attempt to throw light on the present value budget constraint of the government. This restraint means that the government would have to finance its expenditures from the income from current assets (net of debt) and from the resources contributed by current and future generations. To the extent that the current generation pays less (net of transfers) to finance the transactions of the government, the burden will be shifted forward and will have to be borne by future generations. If this burden is regularly shifted forward, then the debt will grow and, over a period of years, if no discretionary unilateral action is taken by the debt holder to forgive the debt, it could reach a stage of default and constitute a major financial crisis. Some city governments in Europe and the United States, as well as some heavily indebted countries, have experienced such a crisis.

Essentially, the system of generational accounts consists of the following elements: (1) value of the future purchases of goods and services by the government, (2) value of future taxes to be paid by existing genera-

---

[8]See Kotlikoff (1992), p. 12.
[9]See United States, Office of Management and Budget (1994), pp. 29–31.

tions, (3) value of the taxes to be paid by future generations, (4) value of the transfers received by existing generations in the future, (5) value of the transfers received by future generations, (6) government debt, (7) value of government assets that yield income in the future, and (8) a discount rate so as to reduce all the values indicated in the preceding steps to the present (that is, at the time of calculation). The present value budget constraint, according to this approach, is that the present value of the government's future purchase of goods and services cannot exceed the sum total of the future taxes paid by current and future generations (net of transfers in each case) and income from the assets net of debt.

To facilitate calculation, the present value of goods and services is computed on the assumption that present policies will continue without any change. This estimate minus the resources paid by the existing generation (net of transfers) and the present value of assets (net of debt—this could be a negative figure in some countries where debt levels are very high) indicates the burden to be borne by future generations. Calculations made for the United States suggest that the generations born after 1993 are likely to make payments 126 percent higher than those born in 1992, while for Norway the comparable figure would be about 69 percent and for Italy (on the basis of data computed for 1990), it could be two or three times larger than the U.S. figure. Basically, however, generational accounts show the aggregate amount (the difference between the present value of government purchases of goods and services minus the future tax payments by existing generations (net of transfers) and income from current assets (net of debt)). This aggregate amount is a single number and cannot be divided among the various taxes or the wide variety of transfers.

The concept of generational accounts, while attractive in some ways, has several obvious limitations.[10] Even family budgets are done on an annual, if not on a much shorter-term basis. Although the conclusions to be drawn into the next generation may be self-evident and compelling, the present generation may tend to think and concentrate (without necessarily contributing to the hedonistic philosophy of Omar Khayyam) on the present rather than on the unborn tomorrow.[11] This may very well be the approach of governments that are in a state of continuous fiscal crisis. Another flaw of the methodology is that it ignores the beneficial impact of

---

[10]Haveman (1994) offers a well-reasoned critique of the Generational Accounts Proposals.

[11]Goode and Steuerle (1994) point out that rational people will take *some* (emphasis in the original) account of what they expect to do in the future but how far ahead and how accurately they will look are problematical. Goode and Steuerle add that "life time planning is limited by myopia, uncertainty, and lack of access to credit during periods of low income. Economists differ on the validity of the life cycle theory of behaviors, and the evidence is mixed" (p. 1031).

public expenditures, and the calculation of the present value of the net assets of the government may not do full justice to the long-term benefits that derive from government expenditures on, among other services, education and health. Furthermore, the methodology neglects to take into account the dynamics of the population, the economy, and the future policies of the government. The choice of the discount rate, as in the cost-benefit analysis, is crucial because of its effect on the calculations. In effect, this methodology seeks to place the policymakers' faith in the analysts' arbitrary choice of rate. It could well lead to a revival of allegations about the tyranny of assumptions over the intuitive approaches of the less quantitative genre of the policymakers.

Even as a foundation on which to base policy decisions, the value of generational accounting is dubious. It can indicate only the broad contours of a problem and may not offer any advantages over the vast array of analytical devices available to a policymaker. The most myopic of fiscal policymakers realize that future generations may have to bear larger burdens once the difference between the rates of growth of revenues and expenditures becomes significant. Also, in contrast to the accrual method of accounting, which relies more on facts and details and is management oriented, generational accounts can serve, at best, only as analytical inputs primarily because of the aggregate nature of the analysis and the imputations involved. These accounts may, however, motivate a policymaker to pay more attention to, among other issues, intergenerational equity. No single aggregate can replace the complexity and subtlety of the details of budgets and accounts. Haveman (1994, p. 96) concludes that, "although certain of the tabulations provided by generational accounting have proved interesting, provocative, and worthwhile, the notion that generational accounts should replace the annual public budget is quite unjustified." It is a reasonable assessment.

3

Cost Measurement, Accounting Standards, and Other Issues

Continued fiscal austerity over the years has diverted the debate from the allocation of resources to the measurement and containment of costs within government. This diversion has led to a more detailed investigation into the approaches to costing in government and the ways in which they could be refined. At the same time, the role of accounting discipline in governments and public bodies needs to be defined, the techniques of cost measurement specified, and appropriate standards set forth for the purpose. Although the emphasis on measuring costs has received an additional impetus during recent years, governments have been concerned with determining costs, even if selectively, for a number of years.[1] For example, they have traditionally estimated the costs of irrigation projects, multipurpose river valley projects, and, in industrial countries, major defense projects before making budget decisions. Cost estimation was mostly limited to new investments and new projects and was covered under the broad rubric "investment planning." But such investments, even at the best of times, represent only a fraction of the total activities of public bodies. Although the rationale for ascertaining costs always existed in government operations, it has received deliberate attention in government circles only for the past three decades.

Before that, the primary purpose of accounting in government was to provide a detailed record of the transactions that took place. The current debate, which will prevail until a satisfactory methodology for cost measurement is developed, evolved for the following reasons: First, the fiscal

---

[1]Economists have been more concerned with costs and gains associated with the substitution ratios if voluntary exchanges were to occur. In such an exchange, there is little concern for the third party, and each one will make himself better off without making someone else worse off. This postulate, also known as Pareto optimality, and its relevance for policymaking in regard to the allocation of resources has been the primary focus of economists. It is recognized that this postulate does not offer unambiguous guidance for policymaking and that personal preferences and judgments continue to play a major role. It is also recognized that each resource has alternate uses and is best employed where its yield is the highest relative to the opportunities available. This approach of opportunity costs has paved the way for the application of cost-benefit and other related quantitative techniques of analysis that explore the available alternatives.

austerity experienced during recent years has made governments examine new operations more closely, so that programs that are not viable can either be scaled down, reformulated, or abandoned. (Indeed, this has been the basis for the introduction of the triennial budget system in Sweden.) Ascertaining costs is implicit in this approach, for without such an assessment, policymakers cannot choose between the merits of one program and the claims of others.

Second, costs have become the overarching theme of accountability. The electorate, although aware of the services provided by public bodies, is more interested in knowing the extent of waste, inefficiency, and fraudulent misuse of government resources. Accountability is now interpreted in terms of provision of services at a specified cost and quality in a given period. Third, a major part of government outlays is now devoted to the provision of subsidies (to the manufacturing sector regardless of ownership) and to the reimbursement of expenses incurred by a third party (as in the case of medical care, where a doctor who is not an employee of the government provides a service to a private citizen, who is then reimbursed by the government). These transactions require, at a minimum, some ex ante basis for calculating costs, which thus play a more extensive role in policymaking. It is incumbent on the accounting system to provide the basic data for the calculation of costs.

Because cost measurement has its origins in commercial practices, it is appropriate to review the development of approaches used in the commercial world. Trends in government accounting are then discussed, and, in this context, the relevance for the government of recent developments in the commercial sector is considered.

Commercial Practices

Practices in the commercial world provide ample evidence to support the conventional adage about continuity and change. At each stage of development, there was a systemic response to new challenges and tasks. The history of commercial accounting shows three broad phases after the introduction of double-entry bookkeeping: management accounting, cost accounting, and what is now known as activity accounting. Each phase illustrates the response of the accounting discipline to the changing technologies of manufacturing and the related industrial organization framework. It would appear that each phase held sway for some time, and, when industrial technology changed, the patterns of production changed, and accounting had to change to maintain its relevance.

Before organized entrepreneurship, transactions took place in the market between owner-entrepreneur and individual buyers, and success was measured in the number of daily transactions.[2] As transactions grew and manufacturing activity expanded, longer-term arrangements had to be made for hiring workers and procuring raw materials. As a result, prices, which were readily obtained in the earlier era through the market, now had to be calculated by estimating labor and material and the efficiency with which they were used. Managers became overseers of these operations and needed accounting information that was somewhat distinct from the annual balance sheets to assist them in monitoring daily activities. Toward this end, simple analytical measures, such as cost per hour, unit, or worker, were devised. Later, as processing industries came into the picture (such as railways), accounting had to generate data on cost per mile and related indicators. Management accounting measures were thus designed to aid in the day-to-day monitoring of activities but not to measure overall profits, which continued to be a separate activity.

In due course, and with rapid changes in the industrial and processing technology, more detailed and specific measures were needed than were being provided under the management accounting system. In particular, the growing inventories of both raw materials and finished products, as well as the distribution of staffing costs (overheads), created the need for cost accounting, whose purposes were to ascertain internal opportunities for improvement and to identify those activities that generated a higher return. Inventory costing, a procedure that permitted the separation of production expense from the cost of manufactured product inventories, developed from this need. Supplemented by methods aimed at determining and distributing overhead costs, inventory costing has become a dominant part of commercial accounting during the past several decades and continues to occupy an important place in the commercial world.

This overall system of management accounting is now considered obsolete. Johnson and Kaplan (1987, p. 1) argue that the information generated by the system "is too late, too aggregated, and too distorted to be relevant for managers' planning and control decisions." They maintain that the reports do not help managers reduce costs because of the time spent on explaining the variations in cost rather than on looking into the technological parameters of their operations. Moreover, the system fails to reflect accurate product costs in that it is based on simplistic and arbitrary methods. Furthermore, because of innovations in production tech-

---

[2]The developments discussed here are based on the detailed description provided in Johnson and Kaplan (1987), pp. 6–14.

nology with just-in-time inventory of raw material deliveries and with a reduced role for personnel (and thus relegating to the background the issue of overhead costs), the overall relevance of management accounting has become fragile. It is also argued that the existing systems of management accounting force managers to be more short term oriented and to treat all cash outlays as expenses for the period in which they were incurred, ignoring future benefits. In short, accounting design should not be left exclusively to accountants, but should also involve engineers and operating managers.

A result of the continued efforts of accountants and technology-oriented operational managers is the emergence of the cost management system.[3] This system explicitly recognizes the transformation that has taken place on the manufacturing floor, which is now dominated not by labor (which hitherto, as noted above, was the main area of attention of cost accounting) but by robotics, computer-aided designs, and flexible manufacturing systems. The changes in technology imply that attention needs to be paid more to growing engineering and data-processing costs than to the decelerating labor and inventory components of costs. It is contended that traditional systems of cost accounting are not only inadequate in the current technological setting, but, if used, they could contribute to distortions in decision making. For example, the allocation of overhead costs on production volume could only encourage excess inventories.

The new technology implies a need for coordinated functioning among the various divisions in the manufacturing unit as well as among the suppliers that provide the inputs. In this context, the role of accounting, it is argued, should not be limited to providing historical data, but should be proactive in managing enterprises and, more significantly, in reducing costs so that enterprises can compete and survive in the marketplace. For this purpose, an integrated cost management system (CMS) has been developed. The CMS has four major elements. The first, which recognizes that resources are often used wastefully, entails estimating costs unrelated to the value added of a product. Because value is added only when a product is being processed, this system attempts to eliminate costs that do not add to the quality of the product, for example, storage costs incurred at the various stages of production. Essentially, the CMS seeks to identify the factors that contribute to the overall costs and to reduce these costs so as to streamline the production process.

The second element of the CMS involves activity costing, which also provides the conceptual underpinning to the design of the system. This

---

[3]The discussion is based on Berliner and Brimson (1988) and Brimson (1991).

concept recognizes that determining the activity level of a business links investment management, cost accounting, and performance measurement. As in government operations, the basic goal is to classify the activities of a firm by function, activity, task, and information elements that broadly represent how work is divided into meaningful blocks. (This classification is comparable to the classification of government transactions into functions, programs, activities, and cost elements.) Activity accounting seeks to associate cost and performance with an activity. Here again, as is traditional, costs comprise direct labor, material, technology, and other identifiable costs (these are comparable to the traditional categories of direct and indirect costs). Unlike in traditional systems, in the activity accounting approach overhead costs are calculated with reference to the consumption method, that is, actual materials or resources consumed.

Thus, the volume-based overhead absorption is replaced by a series of *cost-driver* rates for the activities that comprise the overheads of the enterprise. A cost driver is defined as anything that has a direct influence on the costs and performance of an enterprise. For example, with reference to materials management, material handling is viewed as an activity and each identified stage of material handling as a cost driver. From this, a cost rate *per material movement* can be derived and applied to individual product lines. The costs so identified can be used for investment management so that alternative activities that have potential for a higher rate of return can be identified. This accounting approach also assists in cost analysis and containment in that it illustrates how resources have actually been used.[4] In contrast to traditional methods that focused on describing and controlling inputs as a way of reducing cost pressures, this method seeks a more direct relationship between costs of resources and their purpose. It also establishes links between costs and performance. From the point of view of the enterprise, however, the usefulness of this application lies in its emphasis on identifying and measuring the contribution or impact of each cost driver.[5]

---

[4]For a more detailed discussion, see King, Lapsley, Mitchell, and Moyes (1994), pp. 143–59.

[5]The specific application of this approach to a processing company like American Express offers an illustration. For years, to meet its income target, the company depended upon reducing its operational costs by reducing personnel. But such reductions have limits, and the company had to look for areas that were not related to human resources. It therefore embarked on re-engineering its operations through three approaches—cost re-engineering (using more efficient processing or reducing some operational stages), structural re-engineering (using fewer plants than before), and strategic re-engineering (which required fundamental changes in how the work was performed). Together they contributed to substantial savings. (These measures are comparable to cutting staff, shedding activities, and restructuring the public sector.) See United States, Joint Financial Management Improvement Program (1994a).

The third element of the CMS refers to target costs, which are used to calculate the price that will enable a product to capture or retain a market share. Such targets represent the goals to be achieved through selective reductions in the various activity costs, and detailed activity costs and related strategies are essential.

The fourth element of the CMS entails improving the traceability of costs to management reporting objectives. The CMS recognizes that, in the context of advanced technology, when cost estimations are far off the mark, the consequences for the operations can be serious. It is important that the costs determine the cause and effect relationship and facilitate product costing. This function exemplifies the limitations of the traditional direct and indirect costs. The CMS seeks instead a more precise relationship between cost-driver aspects, operational targets, and management objectives.

The CMS represents the cutting edge of thinking in commercial accounting and, as a response to changing production and managerial styles induced by advanced technology, it shows a greater degree of adaptability and anticipates a future dominated by computer-driven technologies. The system has not, however, been adopted universally. The limited application can be ascribed not to any major conceptual drawback, but mostly to the detailed operational studies that need to be undertaken before the system can be introduced.

Government Approaches

Government accounting, until the early 1950s, was concerned with compiling appropriation accounts so as to provide the legislature and the public with an account of funds collected and spent and the administrative agencies on which they were expended. There was little concern for costs except to estimate them before approving new policies or projects. These estimated costs served as benchmarks of the amounts likely to be appropriated and were more in the nature of back-of-the envelope calculations. They had little value for either monitoring or control purposes, and once policies and projects were approved and included in the budget, the appropriated amounts became the anchors to which the traditional framework of process-related payment control was attached. Into this languid process wafted a fresh breeze in the form of performance budgeting.

Although performance budgeting had been in operation since the early 1920s at the local government level, it came into greater prominence in the 1950s when it was applied to the federal government in the

United States. This approach to budgeting was influenced not by the tradition of public administration, but by management theories and cost accounting. It required (1) an advance program of work, (2) a classification of government activities into functions ("a major division of the total organized effort of government, the purpose of which is to provide a distinct and public service"), programs (a segment of a function that has a measurable major "end" objective), activities (a division of programs into homogeneous types of work), and cost elements or the objects on which expenditures were incurred, and (3) efficiency indicators, including, where possible, measurement of activities.[6] While performance budgeting consists of several elements, those described hereafter are most relevant to the discussion on accounting.

Following the classification of government transactions, the new system basically envisaged two types of accounting orientation—responsibility accounting and cost funding and analysis. Under the former approach, all outlays were charged to a responsible organization as applied costs for its uses. The responsibility costs thus sought to indicate the outlays and results of operations by organizational unit by linking costs of inputs and outputs, or accomplishments. Cost funding and related analysis provided the means by which the underlying responsibilities and, more significantly, costs were arranged, allocated, and summarized. They provided the requisite activity identifications in that the costs of each activity, however measured, were shown separately, in turn providing a continuing linkage for budget allocations, payment and accounting, performance monitoring, and, at a later date, evaluation. Within this broad framework, a distinction was made between operating costs and cost accounting that would apply primarily to construction projects and works. Since performance budgeting did not distinguish between current and capital budgets, the distinction between operating costs and cost accounting was not real but a convenient means of denoting the area of primary applicability. Thus, cost accounting was applied to medical services even when there was no capital outlay. The data showed both operating costs and net service cost. The operating costs mostly referred to outlays on personnel and related administrative expenses. Cost accounting practices in turn distinguished between direct and indirect costs. The former referred to those that could be uniquely applied to a program or a service center and typically included costs of labor and material. The latter included, in principle, costs that could not

---

[6]For a more detailed discussion of this and related systems and their features, see Premchand (1969 and 1983) and United Nations (1965).

be identified with any single project or service but were utilized by more than one cost center and covered costs of selected supplies, equipment, and service facility shops. Costs of service facility shops were calculated on the basis of use of the common facilities or equipment for the project.

Cost funding, in the event, is largely a process of allocating indirect costs to specific programs and projects. Supplementing these approaches, the system envisaged the calculation of standard and average costs. The standard costs represent the best estimate of what each component of the service, or the cost center, should cost on a per unit basis if the organization operates efficiently. Similarly, average costs are also estimated with reference to unit costs of each activity over a period of time and thus provide an indication of movements in the costs. The standard costs set a target for the organizations and were used in conjunction with average costs to monitor the actual costs, variations from the standards, and reasons for variations and to set in motion the forces aimed at rectifying excessive variations.

The implementation of performance budgeting, however, was not successful. Apart from the difficulty of implementing radical reforms in government organizations, the argument that the government was more concerned with providing a service than with recovering costs fully also resurfaced. But as fiscal crises continued, and as other avenues for mobilization of resources were being exhausted, attention turned to measuring and containing costs—the elements that constituted the core components of performance budgeting. Although performance budgeting itself is no longer advocated but is being introduced in different forms in governments, it nonetheless opened new doors on awareness of costs in public organizations.

Despite this awareness, experience shows a sharp divide between developing and industrial countries in their approaches to ascertaining costs. It is instructive to consider briefly the experiences of the United Kingdom, the United States, and developing countries as a group. Before considering these experiences, however, it is useful to recall the distinction between cost containment and cost measurement. The former refers to the recent reductions in expenditure allocations. Governments confronted with resource shortages traditionally maintain pay scales even when they are due to be revised to reflect inflation levels (wage freeze); freeze or even reduce staffing levels through attrition or employee buyouts (early retirement with suitable augmentation in severance benefits); deferral or reduction of capital projects; limitations on running costs or operational costs of programs; or "caps" or ceilings on expenditure levels. These measures represent efforts to contain expenditure growth. In some cases, some of these measures, such as freezes in pay and staffing, can even contribute to selective reductions in costs without affecting the quantity and quality of goods and services provided. Cost measurement reflects the relationships between inputs and outputs, and cost containment refers to maintaining outputs while reducing inputs.

Cost measurement in the United Kingdom received little attention (except for capital projects) until the mid-1960s. Influenced in part by the newly ushered in planning, programming, and budgeting (PPB) systems in the United States, the Fulton Commission in the United Kingdom (1968) that reviewed the working of the government recommended that financial management be improved by taking into account the skills of modern management accounting. But, neither this recommendation nor the 1976 Melville-Burney report,[7] which recommended the establishment of an accounting service in government, sought to define management accounting and its role in the government. As a result, confusion between the new managerialism that was introduced in government during the 1980s and traditional management accounting exists today.[8]

Cost measurement in the United Kingdom occurred in three stages: First, in the wake of the application of variants of PPB systems, efforts were made to develop what were then known as functional costs, broadly comparable to the total outlays for a given function. The purpose was to gather together all the outlays that were scattered throughout the budget and to estimate the costs of selected programs, particularly in the defense sector. This process yielded place to the second stage, familiarly known as "running costs"—which reflected the operational costs of a program and thus included, in addition to the wage component, related expenses on the goods and services that formed the necessary complement of a program. This category was introduced more as an instrument to provide flexibility to managers (as part of the financial management initiative) and less as a device for measuring costs, much less for containing them. These costs merely reflected the financial flows for a program during one year and did not include either the capital component or the accrued overheads.

The third stage refers to the introduction of performance measures, and, as an integral part of this effort, costs were computed for selective

---

[7]For a review of these developments, see Likierman (1994).

[8]The new managerialism refers to hands-on professional management, explicit standards and measures of performance, emphasis on output control, greater competition in the public sector, stress on private sector styles of management practices, and emphasis on greater discipline and parsimony in resource use. For a detailed discussion of the conceptual and practical aspects, see Hood (1991) and Premchand (1994).

operations and used extensively as a basis for budgeting and budget implementation. Most of the performance measures continue to be oriented to the physical aspects of the work load, while, in some sectors, such as health and defense, more vigorous efforts have been or are being made to formulate costs. The need to develop cost measures in the health sector was viewed as particularly acute in view of the preponderant role of reimbursement techniques for compensating doctors and clinics outside the government for services provided. It should also be noted that cost accountancy efforts remain separate from the regular financial accounting operations.[9]

In the United States, too, application of cost accounting has gone through various stages of development, beginning with the development of guidelines in the area of major construction and river valley projects. These efforts received additional impetus, over the years, through the introduction of performance budgeting and PPB systems, which also emphasized the measurement of costs. As a result of these efforts, most agencies in the government have developed cost measurement techniques for purposes of budget formulation and implementation. A survey of existing practices by the U.S. General Accounting Office (GAO) shows that cost information is used primarily for program or activity management, selectively for purposes of performance measurement, and infrequently for allocation of overhead costs.[10] Moreover, no uniform standards currently exist although they are being developed by the U.S. Federal Accounting Standards Advisory Board.[11] In addition, it also appears that, in some cases, there is a schism between external reporting of costs and internal management requirements and that some agencies find the external reporting requirements to be contrary to their internal requirements. In such cases, managers may be merely paying lip service to the system. Moreover, the GAO review also shows that, in several cases, cost accounting was undertaken as a separate effort and was not always linked to the general ledger system.

In developing countries, as noted earlier, accounting systems have not been geared to measuring costs or, therefore, to providing information on costs either to the legislature or to the public. Their primary purpose continues to be the provision of an account of funds received and spent. The rationale for such spending and the costs incurred have not been

---

[9]The picture will change significantly once accrual accounting is introduced fully as is proposed to be done by the end of the century.

[10]See United States, General Accounting Office (1990a).

[11]According to the U.S. Office of Management and Budget (1993), p. 57, these standards are expected to be issued and applied during 1995–97.

included in their purview. Even in countries that have introduced double-entry bookkeeping and where extensive computerization has taken place, such as Chile, little progress has been made in the measurement of costs.

The preceding discussion shows that in both industrial and developing countries, cost measurement has yet to secure a foothold in the overall accounting system. Organizationally, cost accounting and financial accounting remain two separate streams of activity. In some cases, the former is undertaken as an ad hoc exercise and may not be materially dependent on the general ledger system. When systems are centrally designed, they may not reflect the interests of the user and, conceptually, may leave much to be desired. What are described as costs represent, in fact, the financial flows during a year and do not take into account the considerable overhead costs. They may also not include the cost of services provided by other government departments. Finally, the classifications used in most accounting systems today may be so broad that they do not shed light on the factors contributing to expenditure growth or on the impact of the relative price effect. Therefore, information compiled on costs has several limitations, which are further accentuated during inflationary periods. These limitations explain why cost control played a minor role in expenditure management in governments. However, without cost control, the effectiveness of the accounting system is limited.

Relevance of Commercial Practices

Every organization, whether or not it sells its services, has an obligation to ascertain its costs so as to minimize the burden on the taxpaying public. Although there are fundamental differences between governments and the commercial world in terms of motives for providing goods and services and in recovering costs, there is little difference in the estimation or measurement of costs. Cost estimation as practiced commercially may need adjustment in its application to government. The major difference between a government and a commercial organization, a manufacturing one in particular, is that in the latter, production reflects an engineering design, is easily identifiable, and lends itself to precise measurement of costs. In governments, the administrative process is more ambiguous, and there may not always be a match between tasks, power, and responsibility. The three most important factors contributing to higher costs in government are time, overstaffing, and acquisition of

Diagram 3. Time and Costs in Government Operations

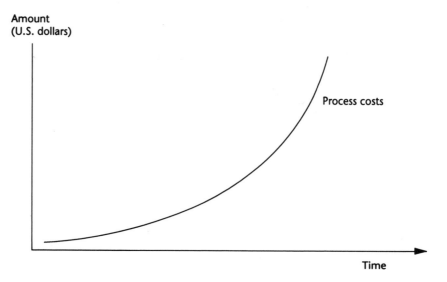

more materials than may be indicated by the tasks to be performed. The time factor in governments is illustrated in Diagram 3.

Evaluations undertaken by governments and international organizations show that projects and programs tend to take longer than initially estimated and that final costs bear no resemblance to the estimates made at the time the project was considered. The extended time may be due to a lack of finances or key materials, extended interdepartmental consultations, and associated process costs. Second, experience shows that government is a major employer, hiring people not because they are needed to provide the services, but because they have to be found employment.[12] Third, materials are often acquired and then lost or not accounted for. In some countries, the loss of acquired materials far exceeds the quantities that are eventually put to use. Costs do not appear to be any lower when services being financed by the government budget are contracted out to be performed by others.

Governments are not unaware of the waste and spiraling costs, which have become endemic in public organizations, that are unrelated to the value added. Indeed, any budget speech, randomly chosen, would contain a passage about the need to avoid waste and to be economical,

---

[12]One of the major factors contributing to higher costs in government is the excess unused capacity. This leads to higher overheads. Cost accounting should help the identification of this element.

efficient, and effective in the use of resources. Although these themes have long dominated the financial management scene, their continued persistence suggests that exhortations do not necessarily contribute to tangible results. Identifiable actions are linked to the introduction of necessary systems, techniques, and improved operating methods. Moreover, what is needed is a strategy aimed at securing an understanding of the dynamic factors that affect cost behavior so that substantive, as opposed to symbolic, factors can be addressed.

The need for improvement in the methods employed in government is clear. In this context, the cost management system appears to be particularly relevant. But, like all applications of commercial approaches to government operations, this system, too, could be objected to on conceptual and practical considerations, as has happened in the past.

A more detailed analysis of the components of the CMS shows that governments and commercial organizations are more similar than they appear to be at first sight (see Table 9). The primary differences are found in manufacturing and in the delivery of services. But government and commercial financial management have other elements in common. For example, unit costs were specified for several years as norms to be achieved by agencies in all former centrally planned economies. Those norms, however, were more abused than used primarily because they were often arbitrary and had questionable empirical underpinning. Furthermore, because the norms were imposed from the outside, agencies complied with them only nominally. In contrast, under the CMS, the role of each cost driver can be identified and measured, and ways to address deviational behavior are outlined. Cost drivers would transform the way in which financial managers work in governments.

Financial managers traditionally viewed budgetary allocations as a handout and considered it their role to spend it in an orderly way. The CMS, however, makes managers responsible for delivering services within specific cost estimates. The applicability of the CMS to government is more wide ranging than is normally perceived; for example, it has been applied to the Internal Revenue Service in the United States. In hospitals, the CMS has had a more extended application, and the cost-driver analysis has been used advantageously to analyze patient movement (appointment, X rays and other radiological tests, film processing, reporting, and review) and to estimate the costs of hospitalization, nursing care, ambulatory services, and a host of related activities. The results of these analyses have contributed to new treatment design, customer profitability, and overall improved care. Thus, the CMS is a significant innovation with considerable potential for government use

Table 9. Application of Cost Management System

Component	Commercial Application	Government Application
Processing costs	These are applied to identify non-value-added costs so that they can be eliminated. These can include time, money, and resources.	Although not engaged in manufacturing, governments have considerable overheads, largely associated with policy formulation and implementation. In several cases, there is a mismatch between oversight and implementation responsibilities.
Activity analysis and costing	These activities are needed to determine costs and performance accurately. Costs can be estimated for both administrative and manufacturing activities.	The activity classification originated in performance budgeting that was primarily applied to public organizations. The intent is common to both government and commercial organizations.
Cost-driver analysis	In its pure form, this analysis identifies activities that influence the cost and performance of subsequent activities. It is supplemented by technology accounting, which identifies all technology costs. The intent is to improve the manufacturing process by eliminating defective parts at an early stage.	This has not been applied in government in the form in which it is applied in the commercial world primarily because of the absence of technology and manufacturing of products. But value engineering, applied in industrial countries, in a way refers to this phenomenon. Value engineering refers to systematic efforts to substitute less expensive items for more expensive ones and to find ways to reduce the costs of carrying out specific tasks. Of late, value engineering is experiencing a revival in the United States.
Target costs	These costs are specified so that products can be manufactured within specified levels, and market shares retained or enhanced.	Although governments are not concerned with market share, their concern for the stabilization of the economy has frequently contributed to the specification of expenditure caps, or ceilings. These, properly formulated and judiciously implemented, are the equivalent of target costs.
Relating costs to performance and management objectives	This is done to determine how efficiently work is being carried out and to ascertain the impact of any policy or technical measure on quality, cost and time, and the product.	Although performance measures have come into greater use in governments during recent years, they are geared to serve the same purpose as in the commercial world, namely, how the policies are being implemented. This is valuable for rendering accountability.

and is likely to play a dominant role in government accounting for the foreseeable future.

Capital Charge

In the case of private sector operations, investors receive dividends, and lenders receive interest on loans made. Regardless of ownership, the state gets the proceeds of income or corporate taxes (unless otherwise specifically exempted). The shareholders invest in an activity with the twin anticipation of receiving a dividend as well as a prospective increase in the share value, which tends to rise along with the growth in the rate of dividends.

When government is the sole investor, there is no feature analogous to capital gains. There is, however, an opportunity cost to the capital. Given its alternative uses, capital is expected to be used or employed where its yield is highest, over a period, relative to the opportunities available. While depreciation, to the extent practiced, provides a recovery of the assets, no systematic recovery of the overall cost of capital has been taken up by the departments in government. Government investment in the operations of its agencies (which is not calculated in the conventional accounting system) is an important element of the total cost of goods and services provided by government. These aspects of sunk capital are also not reflected fully at the time of investment appraisal—that is, when the investment is made—because the techniques of cost-benefit analysis tend to emphasize incremental capital.

Given the substantial government investment (even if depleted over the years by natural causes and neglect of operations and maintenance during periods of fiscal austerity), the question is: What can the accounting system do to promote a full awareness of all costs governments incur in the provision of services? Specifically, how can the cost of capital be recognized and recovered? It is in this context that the practice of the Government of New Zealand and the proposal of the Government of the United Kingdom are relevant.[13] These envisage a depreciation (principally a measure of the use of an asset, its wearing-out use, passage of time, or technological obsolescence) and a capital charge for the unremunerated capital employed. Thus, the operating cost statement, recommended for use in the Government of the United Kingdom, includes provision for cost of capital:

---

[13]See United Kingdom (1994a), and, for New Zealand, McCulloch (1992).

Department Operating Cost Statement

	Amount
Paybill and associated staff costs	
Nonpay administration costs	
Depreciation	
Cost of capital	
Nonrecurring administration costs	
Total operating costs	

Source: United Kingdom (1994a).

In New Zealand, this cost is known as the capital charge rate, and the total capital charge is explicitly shown as an expenditure item in the budget of departments. The capital charge is calculated as the department's charge rate multiplied by its capital base. This process recognizes that the charge rate has two components: (1) operating returns from using the investment in the current year, and (2) expected gains or increases in returns in future years from continued holding of the investment. The former is realized on the assumption that a policy of full cost recovery will be followed each year, while the capital charge is a cash payment that is to be taken into account in computing the costs to be recovered. The capital charge rate is determined, annually, as the difference between the nominal cost of capital minus the expected gains in government holdings. This net rate is expected to ensure that the costs of a department correspond with its revenues during each accounting period. The capital charge is assessed twice a year on the basis of the reported value of assets included in the half-yearly and yearly balance sheets.

The capital charge system, which may still be considered to be in its infancy, is not without intrinsic problems. First, it may have some unintended distortionary effects in that, because human resources are excluded from the computation of the capital base, the allocation of resources between physical and human resource may be affected. Second, private sector practices are not fully applicable to government. In private sector practice, the risk factor in capital asset pricing is taken into account but is extremely difficult to compute for public operations. Third, the mere fact that a capital charge is included does not necessarily oblige a department to undertake full cost recovery. The department may often be engaged in providing many services, some of which may aim to recover full costs while others may seek to recover more or less depending on the market situation. The aggregate indicators in such a situation do not fully indicate the extent of cross-subsidization.

The capital charge should be seen as one of the many elements that need to be taken into account in establishing and operating a cost management system. It is important for the government to ascertain what factors are contributing to cost increases and how those factors may be brought under its control. In this context, it is essential that systems be established to facilitate the assignment of costs to outputs. These mechanisms should make it easier to trace costs directly, assign costs on a cause-and-effect basis, and allocate costs consistently. These include assigning indirect costs, of which the capital charge is an important (and hitherto neglected) one that merits explicit consideration. Cost consciousness or cost recovery cannot occur in the absence of a cost management system. The introduction of such a system should be the primary task of those engaged in formulating policies to improve government accounting.

Foreign Aid Accounts

Before moving to a consideration of the accounting standards, it is essential to consider some important areas that need to be addressed. The accounting of foreign aid is one such area that has gained considerable importance in recent years for both donors and recipients. While the amount of aid extended by donors may not constitute a significant share of their respective budgets, total aid received from various countries and international financial institutions forms a significant portion of the recipients' budgets. In some cases, the share exceeds 30 percent and has a crucial role in fiscal policy formulation and implementation and, as a consequence, in the budget and accounting systems of the country. This increasing role, while reflecting the sphere of shared decision making and responsibilities among donors and recipients, also illustrates the growing demand for accountability and an improved basis for internal management.

Foreign aid covers a wide variety of transactions, including capital assistance, technical cooperation,[14] balance of payments or budgetary sup-

---

[14]Technical cooperation is conceptually broader than technical assistance. The latter generally refers to the provision of personnel, usually engaged in an institution-building activity (and therefore perceived to be additive in nature rather than substitutive for the local personnel), by a donor to a recipient country. The former refers to a broader set of development activities, including training, information exchanges, and the supply of equipment and materials. See Berg and United Nations Development Program (1993).

port, and emergency aid for relief from natural disasters. Aid may be given for projects or activities not related to projects, in the form of food, services, consumable items, cash, or equipment, or in the form of loans or grants. It may be given directly to the central government or through that government to other levels of government or to statutory organizations, public enterprises, or private organizations on the basis of guarantees provided by government. In some cases, aid (such as for relief from natural disaster) may be administered by an international organization, subcontracted out to a consulting firm (in the case of technical cooperation arrangements), or undertaken by the recipient government within the overall framework of conditions that form part of an agreement.

Accounting issues, which in some ways are derived from the approaches and practices of budgeting, differ for donors and recipients. At the donors' end, aid may be provided through the budget directly, through one of the agencies specifically organized for the purpose, or through an extrabudgetary fund and may take the form of a loan, a grant (when equipment or money is given), or services for personnel paid by the donor but used by the recipient country under a technical assistance program. In addition, the budget includes subscriptions to regional and international financial organizations that have been set up specifically to provide aid to developing countries. More recently, as part of debt-relief packages, donor governments have provided relief by forgoing interest, writing off debt, or deferring repayment. Where funds are provided through the budget, the transactions go through the usual process of review and, in most cases, are subject to legislative approval. Where, however, such aid is given from an extrabudgetary fund, or by an organization owned and controlled by government but outside the ambit of the budget, it may not require legislative approval.

For the donor, accounting is a straightforward exercise in that the value of equipment and services is expressed in current terms of the national currency and is so indicated in the budget. The accounts show both actual outlays and the estimates. Reflecting the growing complexity of foreign aid, three issues that are fairly common to most donor countries have arisen.[15] These are the risk assessment of loans, costs of debt relief, and accounting treatment of loans provided to national governments or regional and international organizations for onward assistance to other countries. It is normally assumed that all loans extended to governments, unless repudiated, are collected. However, sovereign governments have,

---

[15]For a typical illustration of some of these issues, see Canada, Office of the Auditor General (1993). Of particular interest are chapters 10, 11, and 12.

in some cases, unilaterally repudiated repayment responsibility, and, in other cases, external pressures have been exerted to forgo the claims. Thus, the loan portfolio as shown in the government accounts may not reflect the real picture. Donor governments must therefore periodically assess their portfolios and make such adjustments as are warranted. It is also suggested that frequently debt relief that is provided in any of the forms described earlier should be reported to the legislature.

The accounting treatment of loans given as part of aid package raises two issues. First, these loans, which usually carry a low rate of interest and have long periods of amortization, are more like grants. It is therefore argued that they should be considered grants from the outset. In the United States, the national income accounts show these loans as grants. But then, these accounts are distinct from budgets and related appropriation accounts and, unlike the budgets, are not operational or legal. Second, the capital provided by donor governments to regional and international financial institutions does not have any return either in the present or in the future and, as such, is distinct from a government's other capital assets. It is suggested that this distinction should also be properly reflected in the accounts.

Issues for the recipient governments are somewhat more complex, reflecting in part the institutional arrangements. Typically, the central agencies in governments are responsible for coordinating all incoming aid and arranging for its inclusion in the government budget. There are also several spending agencies, each one having many project authorities that are responsible for implementing aided projects. There is considerable divergence in the approaches of the spending and central agencies. The former are more concerned with optimizing foreign aid resources, which they consider to be more easily available than domestic resources. Spending agencies see a convergence between their approaches and those of the donors in that they have a collective interest in furthering the development objectives of the country. Also, the donors may be seeking projects or programs that will give them more visibility, ultimately supplanting domestic agencies by advocating causes that are closer to the donors' own agenda and unstated political ends. Although the central agencies are equally interested in furthering the development objectives of the country, their interest is tempered by the need to maintain a vigilant eye on the absorptive capacity of the economy, its repaying capacity, and the collective impact of aid on the stabilization objectives being pursued.

This divergence in the spending and central agencies' approaches, as illustrated further on, could also induce the spending agencies to seek channels of foreign aid outside the regular budget. In preparing the annual budget, the spending agencies may be inclined to show a higher rate of utilization of foreign aid so as to buttress their demands for the allocation of domestic financial resources. The central agencies, in contrast, may follow more conservative approaches, and the eventual size of annual allocations may be determined jointly by the central agencies, the spending agencies, and the donor. Transactions included in the budget may not necessarily be reflected in the regular accounts and, if they are, they may be maintained as an integral part of satellite accounts that are not within the jurisdiction of the accountant general.

In some countries, separate offices are established either in the finance or in the planning ministry to maintain aid accounts. Further aid given in kind (except food or commodity aid that would generate counterpart funds when sold to the public) may not enter the accounts for the simple reason that no credit or cash transactions pass through either the treasury or the banking system. Discrepancies between the data furnished by donors and those prepared by the central agencies and the accounting authority of the government are therefore likely. Similarly, technical assistance (as distinct from technical cooperation) may be included in the budget although practices across countries are by no means uniform. In India, Kenya, Zimbabwe, and, more recently, Tanzania, for example, the purposes as well as the magnitude of technical assistance are specifically included in the annual budget. But these may not find their counterparts in the annual accounts of the government because the transactions do not pass through the accounts.

The budget may also show the amounts on-lent to regions or public enterprises. Under this approach, the amounts repaid and interest paid may also be shown in the budget. Frequently, the amortization periods and other on-lending terms may be different and, indeed, more stringent than those specified by the donor, to cover the risks involved in such on-lending. Guarantees provided by the government may not always be shown either in the budget or in accounts except when formal procedures of scrutiny are a prerequisite for the provision of such guarantees and related contingent liabilities are shown in the annual accounts of the government.

The amounts included in the budget may be made available to the recipient governments in three ways. Cash grants (in foreign or domestic currency—the latter accrue when the donor retains some of the counterpart funds) may be directly transferred to the credit of the recipient government. In regard to project loans, where adherence to the international competitive bidding procedures is deemed obligatory, either a letter of credit or a reimbursement procedure may be adopted. Under the former, the supplies of equipment may be directly paid by the donor, and no transaction may appear in the account books of the recipient country. The project authority would initiate the requisite administrative actions with the donor, and the transaction would appear only when the donor reports the disbursements made. In some cases, however, the amounts at issue may first be paid out of the consolidated funds of the government and then claimed from the donor. In this case, the transaction would be included in the government accounts from the initial stages as an outflow that is subsequently reimbursed by the donors. This procedure, which is still prevalent, although on a reduced scale, implies greater pressure on domestic finances and may strain cash management. To avoid this stress, some international and regional financial organizations have set up revolving funds through which selective advances can be made and pressures on domestic resources reduced.

The process described above has developed several problems related to the management of foreign aid and accounting. First, numerous problems of coordination among projects and between donors and recipients exist, and decisions about the selection of projects are diffuse and extensively fragmented, hampering the negotiation and utilization of aid. In addition, there is the more philosophical issue of whether aid has been fully transparent and effective. These points form part of a separate discussion and are therefore not covered here.

As for accounting, aid given in kind, including commodity assistance, is generally not included in either the budget or the accounts. Even when it is included, there are substantial differences between the quantity of aid indicated by the donors and that recorded by the recipients. Although some related procedural matters have already been considered, it is essential that they be examined in depth. When formally negotiated with the central agencies, aid given in the form of equipment or other consumables and extended as a grant is usually recorded in the budget. When it is extended directly to the spending agencies or to governmental organizations, it is unlikely to be included in the budget, particularly if the amounts are small. More or less the same could be said about technical assistance. Recipient governments are less than eager to show the full amount of technical assistance in the form of salaries for expatriate personnel, even if paid by the donors, because they appear enormous when converted into local currency. Although the tenets of transparency and accountability demand that aid received be included in the budget, such budgetary presentation may create controversies. These are tempered by recognition of the spillover effects and by expediency. When commodity aid is sold in the market, it generates counterpart funds that become a short-term resource for the government.

The discrepancies in the valuation of aid occur basically for three reasons. First, the coverage of aid may be different between the donor and the recipient. The former may include aid given to public enterprises and nongovernmental organizations that do not form part of the budgetary transactions of the recipient. Second, the goods may be declared at a value lower than that indicated by the donor when they are cleared through customs in the recipient country. Since, in most cases, the aided imports may be duty free, the spending agencies in the recipient governments may not declare the correct market value (in some cases, the scarcity of information contributes to this phenomenon). As the central agencies in the host countries proceed on the basis of customs declaration, the amount of aid may be shown as less than that indicated by the donor. Third, the exchange rates used by donors and recipient countries may be different and may contribute to avoidable discrepancies between the two sources. These tend to be magnified when the aid received is substantial. This very factor of substantiality also makes it imperative that accounting be improved.

While several countries have made a good deal of progress, aid accounting remains a murky area. Two types of improvements are needed. First, a comprehensive aid accounting system needs to be established regardless of political views about including all types of aid in the budget. Such an accounting system, which is best maintained as a satellite account, should indicate total resources received, the pattern of their use, and their contribution to the local economic development effort. Second, there should be a periodic reconciliation of data with each individual donor so that discrepancies can be identified and their origins traced and resolved. This regular dialogue, whose importance cannot be overemphasized, should also address the issues arising from direct purchases funded by donors.

A second problem area in managing foreign aid relates to funds onlent to regional governments and public enterprises. It is argued that neither the budget nor the accounts provide an accurate record of those transactions. This problem stems from the relationship between regional governments and public enterprises on the one hand, and with the donors on the other. During the early years of aid administration, funds were routinely channeled through the central government. Pressure to increase direct contact between these sublevels of government and the donors has since grown although experience has shown that direct contact could weaken the traditional role played by the central agencies in the central government. Often, the terms of on-lending are not specified at the outset, and claims are neither registered properly nor tracked effectively for follow-up action. Furthermore, interest payable may be deferred, written off, or capitalized, and similar treatment may be extended to the principal as well. In the process, both transparency and accountability may be jeopardized, leaving an enduring gap in financial management. It is therefore essential that separate records be maintained as part of the satellite account referred to above.

Finally, the accounting systems at the project level are weak. Frequently, the documentation needed to claim reimbursement from the donor is not maintained properly and, even when it is maintained, documents may not be submitted on time. Inevitably, this has an adverse impact on a country's cash management, which is already, in most cases, under severe stress. In some cases, projects are set up on the basis of partial funding by user charges, but slowness or a lack of eagerness in collecting those charges may also have an adverse impact on the overall financial status of the governments. These problems, in turn, require the installation of adequate accounting systems in the projects. The general ledger system described in earlier sections is a good framework for a satellite accounting system that would address these shortcomings. The satellite accounting system can be maintained either manually or electronically with considerable advantage to all concerned.

Accounting Aspects of Privatization

Since the mid-1980s, privatization has gained acceptance as a major plank of the fiscal policy of governments in most industrial and developing countries. The term privatization is not necessarily restricted to the divestiture, in one form or another, of state-owned enterprises. It also covers the sale of government assets, including property. In both categories, government accounting suffers several shortcomings in the following areas: (1) costs associated with privatization of public enterprises, (2) losses incurred in the sale or divestiture of enterprises, and (3) losses incurred in the sale of government-owned assets other than public enterprises.

The sale of public enterprises is often preceded by the injection of additional capital and debt funding aimed at making the condition of the enterprises more attractive. In addition, certain costs are associated with the use of underwriters, with the provision of sales incentives, with the guarantee of a net return on income after privatization for an indefinite or extended period, and with sales. Generally, these costs are not explicitly estimated and, if they are estimated, they are not given due publicity. In most cases, they are shown in neither the budget nor the accounts. More often than not, sales proceeds are shown in the budget net of these expenditures, adversely affecting both transparency and accountability. An appropriate way to overcome these problems is to show the amounts for each of these transaction groups in the budget and the accounts. While such a presentation may be seen as a self-fulfilling prophecy, these estimates are not about the sale value of either the shares or the enterprise itself but reflect the transaction costs associated with privatization.[16] The public needs to be assured that the transaction costs are reasonable.

A second problem arises when the seller does not realize the full market value of the shares or the enterprise. Experience shows that any of the following practices will result in a gross undervaluation of the enterprise:[17] giving it to workers and managers, selling it to workers and managers, arranging a spontaneous privatization (in which workers and managers find a buyer at a negotiated price that primarily enriches the manager rather than enhancing the value received by the government), or offering vouchers to citizens entitling them to claim shares in an enterprise. This is primarily because the existing accounting systems do not maintain the value of the assets in current market prices but rather at the acquisition or purchase value. This practice illustrates how little weight is attached to accountability in government administration. The appropriate procedure (indeed, it is a normal and logical expectation of the accounting system) would be to maintain a record of the asset in terms of the current market value, which requires an annual updating of the values of all assets.

In addition to enterprises, governments are also selling other types of property that they own, including land, releases from commodity inventories, surplus equipment, and releases from strategic stockpiles of selected nonferrous metals. These sales were a normal part of government activity long before privatization became the cornerstone of government

---

[16]This section is not concerned with the problems of the accounting approaches followed by public enterprises. The general assumption is that they follow commercial accounting approaches. But this is not always correct. In many cases, accounts are organizationally structured (e.g., postal and telecommunications), and it is not always easy to separate the accounts of a commercial entity. Some enterprises may follow only cash-based systems that vary substantially in their content and coverage. These problems are particularly acute in the economies in transition. In these cases, decisions regarding the classification of transactions, the recording of production cost flows, the allocation of costs, depreciation, and amortization were centrally determined, reflecting the needs of the planners rather than of management. Accounts must be extensively restructured if they are to meet the criteria of commercial formats. Further, they involved the concentration of bookkeeping and fiscal regulations in the same standard-setting body. Thus, the budget was largely dependent on revenues generated by the enterprises because accounting rules had a bias that would provide for more tax collections. Lack of external accountability also affected the values assigned in the accounting process, such as those relating to receivables, stocks, fixed assets, and contingent liabilities. For a discussion of these issues, see United Nations Conference on Trade and Development (1993), pp. 25–27.

[17]For discussion with reference to the United Kingdom, see Beauchamp (1990b).

fiscal policies and may also represent a serious undervaluation whose magnitude cannot always be ascertained. Furthermore, because storage costs are not computed, it is difficult to assess the sales option. If government agencies maintained regular balance sheets of assets and liabilities, assessment would be simplified.

Accounting and Performance Indicators

Although performance budgeting as a system did not have a long life in the early 1950s when it was first introduced, many of its elements are now accepted in modern budgetary management. The system recognizes that different agencies perform different tasks and should therefore be delegated adequate power and responsibility to discharge their tasks. This includes the power to use the resources allotted for specific tasks on the assurance that specific outcomes would be generated. The agencies, in turn, must be accountable for delivering services for a set cost and within an agreed time frame. In sum, the system involves the specification of performance indicators in four broad areas: productivity, cost per unit or task, time frame, and budgetary outcome and effectiveness.

These areas are generally considered to be part of a management information system, which tends to be counterproductive when designed as a stream of activity separate from, or parallel to, traditional accounting. Because most of the basic data needed for a management information system are drawn from the accounting system, it is appropriate that the latter be strengthened to serve management interests. Accordingly, each organization would need to develop subsystems of accounting. Productivity measurement would involve assessing the relationship between the existing capacity and the services scheduled to be delivered. These services would inevitably differ from one agency to another. Essentially, however, on the assumption that existing technology continues without any major change, productivity measures seek to indicate the average output units per person. Weights are also used to express comparable types of work done in each area on a comparable basis. In addition, the quality of work, such as permissible error rates, is also specified.[18]

Similarly, costs need to be measured and specified in ranges so as to explain the difference between estimated cost and realized actual cost after the contracts have been finalized and implementation completed.

---

[18]For an illustration of these aspects with reference to the United Kingdom and the annual reports submitted by each ministry as part of the annual budget, see Durham (1987).

These cost estimates, as has been noted previously, have become quite sophisticated. In addition to the traditional area of construction, they are prominent in health, education, and entitlement administration. For example, the costs for health care programs are now calculated in detail in the industrial countries for various types of hospital treatment, visits to the physician and dentist, and so on. In the United Kingdom, budget documents for many agencies routinely show the unit costs for various programs for the budget year as well as the forecast years. The reasons for variations are also explained in detail. These provide an organized basis for more purposeful expenditure control.

The budgets also show the time frame for the completion of projects and programs, as well as what may be expected in terms of the achievement of original objectives. The following points must be recognized in devising performance indicators. (1) Each agency has its own unique features of work, objectives, and performance orientation. (2) Most of these features have their origins in the accounting data generated, although a few are bound to be outside the purview of the accounting system. In devising indicators, each agency should involve both the users and the accounting unit at every step of the process. (3) It is essential that these indicators be closely linked with the accounting system so that relevant standards can be developed for government-wide application. Linking the two will create a central point for disseminating information and for using it during the budget process.

Other Issues

Many observers have commented with almost monotonous regularity that accounting information is considerably delayed or received long after it is due or needed. These delays have hindered effective policymaking and the restructuring of the public sector. While a number of factors have contributed to the ineffective operation of the accounting system as a whole, three of them merit consideration. These are (1) systemic issues (other than those discussed earlier), (2) process factors, and (3) the quality and quantity of human resources.

The systemic issues stem primarily from the existence of too many accounts and avoidable suspense accounts.[19] As discussed earlier, the existence of extrabudgetary accounts will not be a major problem as long as

---

[19]The World Bank, in its report (1994a) observed "public spending is difficult to track because of numerous off-budget accounts, the opacity of military budgets, and the financial operations of public enterprises and the banking system (p. 125)."

specific accounting procedures govern their initial compilation and consolidation at a later stage of operations and as long as channels of communication exist between the compiling agency and the central accounting agency. In addition, if these accounts are computerized, then the central agencies have automatic access to these operations on an up-to-date basis. In practice, however, these conditions are not always found, with the consequence that the flow of information is substantially hindered. Indeed, some of these off-budget accounts, which in several cases are operated by the security arm of the government, claim to be outside the purview of the normal accounting system. While some of these claims may be tenable in part, they do not apply to the broad spectrum of funds. The funds may be organized to provide some degree of operational autonomy (and hence flexibility) rather than to avoid the application of government-wide accounting standards. Indeed, such a posture could compromise accountability. It is therefore essential that the continued relevance of these funds be reviewed and efforts made to rationalize them. A balance has to be achieved between accounting convenience and the operational autonomy of the fund managers.

Suspense accounts represent a separate problem. They refer, with some regional variation, to the provisional booking of receipts and expenditures pending final transfer to their intended destination and broadly comprise two types: (1) payment delays (or float) awaiting final transfer to the bank accounts of the government, and (2) accounts maintained in the budget awaiting final transfer to the consumer or original budget allottee. These transactions occur mostly where centralized arrangements exist for the procurement of stores used throughout the government and the operations of the public works department. In these cases, transactions are undertaken by these agencies on behalf of the indenting departments, and suspense accounts arise when the initial payment is either received or made by the central agency and then adjusted against the agency when the orders for stores or works are placed. These adjustments tend to be time consuming and involve large-scale carryovers from one year to the next.

The first type of suspense account can be minimized or, at any rate, the discrepancies between government and monetary accounts can be resolved through improvements in the payments system and through regular reconciliation. The second type of suspense account has been limited in some countries by not allowing separate budgets for the central agencies engaged in the provision of services. In these cases, the client agencies' budgets for stores purchase and public works are transferred at the outset of the year to the central agencies to administer directly. Elsewhere, payments systems have been improved so that the client agencies can pay for and carry the goods. In some countries, however, these suspense accounts persist and are used to circumvent budgetary discipline. For example, in India, the client agencies routinely spend their budget allotments and seek additional funds when demands are received from the central agencies.[20] This can have a substantial, adverse impact on the eventual budget outcome. These problems illustrate that suspense accounts have become cumbersome and have created difficulties in the compilation of accounts. An obvious solution is to minimize the number of suspense accounts while improving the payments system. Such improvements have become imperative because, under the new managerialism, the central departments are obliged to compete with the private sector in providing services to the client departments in government.

Process factors refer to the proximity between policymakers and the individuals responsible for providing accounting information. Accountants are not decision makers on matters of expenditure control but do play an important role in providing consistent and credible information to both the policymaker and the general public. In this respect, fulfillment of the promise has been substantially less than expected, largely because, as illustrated in the previous discussion, of the organizational and process factors involved in the compilation of accounts. The processes adopted are ancient. Responsibilities are extensively fragmented. Operations are governed by outdated regulations. There are competing bureaucracies and a muddle of unenforceable regulations. Even where a computerized system is in place, it remains an information retrieval system and has not brought about major changes in the orientation and the values of the system. The organizational culture remains narrow, in most cases, and accounting is viewed as distant and limited to being a link with audit, and, when operational, legislative committees. A continuation of this role is unlikely to equip government accounting agencies to serve the numerous purposes inherent in the national fiscal management scene in current and future settings. Values and orientation do not, however, change through central command or hope. Change must be effected from within and happens when improvement is made in implementation. Improvement can be brought about through fine-tuning rather than through the imposition of an overall design.

Far too often, the shortcomings of the accounting systems are ascribed to shortages of skilled personnel. Cursory evidence shows that most accounting organizations are adequately staffed but that most of the staff

---

[20]See, for example, Gupta (1993), pp. 85–87 and pp. 117–30.

are engaged in repetitive and elementary tasks that can be performed with greater effectiveness by a personal computer. It is quite likely that if the cost of processing accounting documents were estimated, it would show a persistent increase in overheads, reflecting unused capacity. Furthermore, deploying more personnel without addressing the underlying processes and techniques is unlikely to improve performance. Shortage of skilled personnel is, however, a separate matter. In most governments, staff become accountants by virtue of being employed as such, and very few are trained and qualified. Although when governments switch over to double-entry bookkeeping and maintenance of commercial-type accounts, staff mobility is likely to improve, there will still be a need for intensive staff training at all levels. Moreover, efforts should be made to improve the working relationship of program and finance managers. In the government of the United States, for example, these issues are being addressed through improved communication and intensive training.[21]

Accounting Standards

The preceding discussion shows that elements of government accounting are open to interpretation and that the potential exists for widely differing practices and, ultimately, a lack of coherence between different governments or within a particular country. Standards are needed to secure uniform compliance from government agencies. Standards would also highlight the differences between government and commercial accounting systems and the reasons for the differences. This section is devoted to a discussion of accounting principles and standards, followed by a consideration of the elements that need standardization and a review of other financial management areas in need of improvement. The concluding part deals with the organizational aspects of the specification of standards.

Standards are different from principles. The latter deal, in this context, with the general features and goals of accounting, while the former are more specific and provide the operational basis for agencies to apply in

---

[21]The Joint Financial Management Program in the United States emphasized that the pursuit of wise spending is common to both program and financial managers and that the perception of conflict should yield place to a commitment to collaboration. Toward this end, it was suggested that financial management should be viewed as a career rather than as just a job and that financial management concepts should be incorporated into new employee orientation programs. It also added that the financial managers' performance should include a critical "program response," while the program managers' plans should include a "financial management" element. See United States, Joint Financial Management Improvement Program (1992b).

their day-to-day activities. Principles may indicate that each organization should have an acceptable accounting system that facilitates public disclosure of the financial status of the agency. The system should publish data periodically (annually) that should be simple, verifiable, and comprehensive. The system should be sustainable and should facilitate the matching of sources and uses of funds. The organization expected to give a more material form and sustainable action to these principles should be well structured and cost effective. Although not specifically recognized, cost is an important element. The conversion of these principles into action does not justify unlimited costs. Rather, the costs of compliance should be explicitly recognized and should be taken into account in designing the organization that is to be made responsible for the regular practice of these principles.[22]

The principles need to be accompanied by the specification of standards guiding all aspects of accounting. Without standards, accounting practices would diverge, and it would be difficult to ascertain the status of government finances. Standards are needed to make available information that is "understandable, relevant and reliable about the financial position, activities and results of operations"[23] of the government and its units. Formulation of standards involves identifying issues in each area and determining how to address them. In considering the issues and in evolving the standards, due attention must be paid to user needs. These needs are not homogeneous given the wide diversity among users.

The needs of central agencies tend to be different from those of the spending agencies or the legislature. Essentially, these differences reflect basic distinctions between macro- and micromanagement. Accounting is

---

[22]These principles, which are an expression of general intent, are different from the more specific principles enunciated as part of the Generally Accepted Accounting Principles. These principles include full disclosure, compliance of legal and contractual provisions, operations of funds, distinctions among the various types of assets, enumeration and specification of long-term liabilities, basis of accounting, the capacity of the accounting system to serve the government budgets, classification of revenues and expenditure, and contents of financial reports. They also include accountability, intergenerational equity, reliability, relevance, timeliness, consistency, and comparability. The principles thus combine a statement of general principles and specification of minimum standards.

[23]Mission Statement for the U.S. Federal Accounting Standards Advisory Board. See United States, Federal Accounting Standards Advisory Board (1991). It may be noted in this context that in regard to companies in the private sector (which include public enterprises registered under the Trade or Companies Act), the International Accounting Standards Committee (IASC) has been endeavoring since 1973 to improve financial reports through the development and publication of accounting standards (see International Accounting Standards Committee (1992), and Ernst & Young (1993)). The standards suggested by the IASC are viewed as a benchmark for countries that develop their own requirements and are used by companies and government authorities regulating domestic and foreign companies. Over the years, several standards have been issued, and these are regularly updated to reflect the changing realities.

the common instrument of both. Standards may thus not always be uniform and may, in certain cases, take into account the unique features of an agency. The standards must represent a balance between what is needed and what is practicable. If the latter is substantially different from the former, a phased implementation program may be appropriate. In some cases, the existing standards may need to be replaced or modified, and the need as well as the utility of the proposed standard should be clearly demonstrable. The standards should be clear and viable. Above all, there should be a balance between the costs incurred in developing the standards and the expected benefits. The standards are not substitutes for operations, nor do they consist of forms designed for the purpose of recording data. They provide the rationale, the philosophy, and the objective as well as the meaning for the regular accounting activity in a public entity.

The type of standards needed and their components are illustrated in Table 10. The description should not be considered exhaustive. The applicability of the standards to government and its entities raises two issues. These standards may not necessarily apply to all levels of government. The increasing decentralization of responsibilities implies that most of the tasks that were hitherto performed by the central government would be performed at the provincial, regional, state, and local levels. But a major part of the funding for these tasks may continue to flow from the central government in the form of either shared revenues or block grants. In either event, the lack of congruence between resources and responsibilities makes it imperative to establish standards for operational control and accounting systems at all levels. In a number of industrial countries, separate standards have been set up for various levels of government. In the United Kingdom, local authorities have developed distinct standards that run parallel to those of the private sector. In the United States, many of the standards that are now found at the state and local government levels were developed over a half century by the National Council of Government Accounting (NCGA). Its activities were later absorbed by the Governmental Accounting Standards Board.

Another issue is the applicability of government standards to the state enterprise sector. These enterprises represent a wide variety of organizational forms and include departmental enterprises, companies, and corporations. While the companies are expected to follow commercial accounting standards (as may be specified in the legislation relating to the establishment of companies), the path of departmental enterprises and corporations is less clear. Accounting arrangements for departmental enterprises are usually laid out in the government accounts, while ac-

Table 10. Government Accounting Standards

Category	Description
Financial resources of the agency	The standards should specify the basis, coverage, and features of each of the resources of the agency.
Accounting of the assets	The assets of the agency, including cash, fund balances with the banks, accounts receivable, advances and prepayments, and investments in real assets and financial assets, should be considered in the specification of standards. The valuation of the assets and the procedures relating thereto should be specified.
Accounting of the liabilities	The standards applicable to accounts payable (including interest), other current liabilities, contingent liabilities, and unquantified contingent liabilities should be specified.
Accounting of inventory and other property	Standards relating to inventory, operating materials and supplies, and stockpile materials (where applicable, seized property, commodities, and other related items) must be specified.
Accounting for property, plant, and equipment	This category deals with the standards relating to land (including its valuation principles), general property, plant and equipment of the agency, national monuments, and weapons systems.
Accounting for loans and loan guarantees	These standards deal with the portfolio of credit programs operated by the agency. These transactions include domestic and external loans as well as the implications of guarantees.
Development of cost standards	These specify the elements involved in estimating costs and their treatment. While the broad elements may be applicable to all agencies, some are unique. In addition, some elements, such as the allocation of pensions (where they are fully paid from the regular budget appropriations), interest costs, and properties arising from grants paid to other units or levels of government may pose problems. Similarly, the separation and costing of capital projects may create difficulties in separating human capital from other types of capital.
Performance indicators	The standards deal with such performance measures as work load and other indicators of effectiveness. These indicators differ from one agency to another and may change frequently as the priorities of the agencies change.
Foreign aid accounting	The standards specify the basis of recording, process of reconciliation, and maintenance of records of aid received in kind. These supplement the standards specified for projects.
Fiscal reporting	The standards deal with the objectives of fiscal or financial reporting, the content and periodicity of reports, and the clientele groups that are targeted by these reports. Where physical aspects also need to be reported, the links between financial and physical aspects and the approaches relating thereto are specified.

counting arrangements for corporations are expected to be specified in the relevant legislation. Regardless of their organizational form and the environment in which they function, these entities are primarily engaged in commercial activities, that is, in selling goods and services to the public. It is therefore necessary to envisage standards that are applicable to these entities. They may be the same as those that apply to commercial organizations or may, in some cases, require modification.

Establishing standards for government accounting will involve a departure from the orientation of the accounting systems now in operation in most countries. From maintaining accounting records of appropriations to explaining archaic regulations and conventions, the standards should pave the way for forward-looking systems that will subserve the needs of internal management. The standards represent only one of the pillars of overall financial management. Effective provision of government services requires an overall improvement in the financial management of the public sector. The components of financial management that are in need of strengthening would differ from country to country, and officials in each must articulate a comprehensive government policy about the future direction of financial management.

A cursory review of a sample of countries shows that most developing countries do not have a rational and sustained government policy on financial management in general or on accounting in particular. Meanwhile, new forces have emerged that influence the way governments work. Not grasping these changes and not engaging in the constructive effort of strengthening the government could have an adverse impact that may take even more time to rectify. It is imperative that governments envisage these changes as part of an overall framework for strengthening government financial management. The United States Government, for example, has initiated a five-year plan to revitalize financial management at the federal level.[24] Its plan envisages development in seven key areas: (1) accountability standards, (2) financial management organization (internal relationships between program and financial managers), (3) financial management personnel (strengthening training programs), (4) financial systems (updating software and other electronic data processing (EDP) technology), (5) management controls (internal controls in the agencies), (6) asset management (property management, recovery of loans, etc.), and (7) audit financial reporting (improving the content and timeliness of audited accounting statements). Benchmarks are specified in the plan and are expected to be implemented according to the sched-

---

[24]See United States, Office of Management and Budget (1993).

ule. In a similar way, New Zealand overhauled its financial management through such legislation as the State Sector Act of 1988 (which marked a new era in the relationships between ministers—the political level of decision making—and heads of departments—the administrative level) and the Public Finance Act of 1989 (which revamped the budget and accounting system). Many industrial countries have also initiated organizational and legislative measures to strengthen their systems.[25] Similar efforts are indicated in other countries, where an initiative in this regard is long overdue.

The formulation of accounting standards should be a collective effort. To permit maximum objectivity, it is best undertaken outside the normal functioning of the government by the users of the spending agencies, accounting professionals in the government and the commercial world, economists, and administrators. This group must focus on the requirements of the public and its desire to comprehend governmental activities. The changes are substantial, the tasks are large, and the results are likely to come slowly. The consequences of inactivity could be even more substantial.

---

[25]See Organization for Economic Cooperation and Development (various issues) for a summary of these developments.

4

Liability Management

Notwithstanding hope and prayer, budgetary outcomes often differ from budget estimates. Although one reason for this is the tentative nature of estimates, another reason for discrepancy is that government budgeteers tend to deliberately ignore certain likely developments and hope that every adverse development will be matched by a positive development. It is also pointed out, although conclusive statistical evidence is lacking, that the budgetary outcome is different largely on the expenditure side, while variations on the revenue side, both positive and negative, are generally limited. Partly with a view to addressing this problem, efforts have been made, through the introduction of governmentwide accounting standards, to minimize the expenditure variations between estimates and outcome. While accounting standards in any form, including commercial practices, have several other major aims, their focus on proper recording, valuation, and regular disclosure makes it easier to recognize four types of liabilities—payables, funded, contingent, and unfunded. When accounted for, these liabilities contribute to a budgetary outcome congruent with estimates. This chapter discusses the features of these liabilities and how they are recognized, budgeted, accounted for, and managed.

Payables

In the balance sheet approach to accounting, entries are made on both sides of the register to represent the inflow and outflow of an entity. On the outflow side, there are entries for accounts payable, interest payable, and other funded liabilities. Their counterparts on the inflow side are accounts receivable, interest receivable, and associated categories. In the commercial world, the difference between accounts receivable (which are funds owed by the distributors to the manufacturing company) and accounts payable (which are funds owed by the manufacturing company to its own suppliers) is of considerable importance in determining the magnitudes of working capital. Although the concept of working capital does not have the same applicability in the public sector as in the commercial world, it does influence cash management.

To the extent that the recovery of receivables is slower than expected and given that most payables to public authorities, including interest payable, can be changed at short notice only at great cost to the government's credibility, the need for short-term borrowing may arise. Borrowing, in turn, would affect the overall level of expenditure contributed by interest payments on the amounts borrowed. Recovery of receivables, which is now largely considered in the context of credit management, is not covered here because the focus is on the expenditure side.

Accounts payable by public authorities fall into four broad categories: (1) payment for personnel services in the form of wages, salaries, and associated benefit payments; (2) payment for services and equipment received from other publicly owned organizations and enterprises; (3) payment for services and equipment provided by private sector contractors; and (4) interest payable by the government. The first category often involves payment in the fiscal year following the year in which services are rendered. These transactions are usually covered by the relevant budgetary authority, although in some cases, pending the approval of the new and requisite authority, an interim measure, such as a vote-on-account or a continuing budget resolution, may be approved to carry out the transaction. The second category usually involves payments to public utilities and other organizations that may or may not be owned by the government. Prior to the intensification of privatization efforts, most government accounts payable reflected the amounts owed to water, electricity, transportation, and communication companies. Because governments represent a big buyer of these services, perhaps the biggest, they seem to enjoy some perquisites with the supplier, including delays in payments.

The third category involves transactions with private sector contractors for the supply of equipment, fabrication in major projects (including turnkey jobs), or routine supply of consumables, such as cleaning materials to a government-owned hospital. These transactions are covered by contracts arrived at through a legal process involving open tenders and scrutiny of bids. The contracts also specify the terms and conditions of payment. For major projects, such as those funded by international financial institutions, contractors generally received an advance that serves as working capital, which is then recovered over the period of the contract. The fourth category covers transactions that are usually considered part of public debt management. It is not uncommon for interest payable, when the government is in a period of severe financial crisis, to be capitalized and the debt payment to be rolled over.[1]

How payables are recorded and how they are recognized in the budget for additional funding depend largely on the type of accounting system used in a government. Until recently, many cash-oriented systems based on single-entry bookkeeping did not provide for the recognition of these payables. Now, however, with the massive application of computer technology to record government transactions, facilities exist to permit their explicit recognition. General ledger systems provide for recording budgetary authority and appropriation, apportionments, and the payment status of apportionments. Subsidiary systems can be used to record accounts payable; for example, journal entries are maintained for facilitating a follow-up of accounts payable. The general ledger reflects journal entries liquidated.[2] In some countries, the magnitudes of these transactions in the last week of the fiscal year are significant. Apart from the rush of expenditures usually noted in the last month of the fiscal year, the transactions reflect on the lackadaisical manner in which the budget is implemented for a major part of the fiscal year. Accordingly, some countries stop issuing checks by the third week of the last month of the fiscal year so that accounts can be closed promptly at the end of the year. This does not necessarily mean that there are no payables at the end of the year. A second approach has been to maintain a legally specified complementary, or liquidation, period at the end of the fiscal year. This implies that two sets of books are maintained for a major part of the year—one set for the current year and another for the previous year(s). This approach complicated the maintenance and closing of accounts and their reconciliation with the monetary flows recorded at the paying end, that is, by banks. The practice, which was common in Latin American countries, has largely been abandoned.

---

[1]The settlement of liabilities of the above type may pose problems in systems in which annual lapse of budgeted funds is a common feature. To prevent such lapses, several formal and informal procedures are in vogue. In some countries, capital or development expenditures are carried over to the next year legally. In a few countries, the unspent amounts are revoted to be spent in the following year. In a few cases, the unspent amounts are diverted to personal ledger or deposit accounts to be available for spending during the following year. These measures generally erupt onto the scene during the last part of the fiscal year, when there is a frenetic activity to save the unspent budget allocations. This avoidable rush is largely due to the absence of a well-structured tracking system for monitoring commitments.

[2]In some cases, either as a result of deliberate action or because of transit delays, there may be large amounts in unpaid checks. Technically considered a float awaiting payment by the banking system, unpaid checks could pose a major policy issue. Similar is the case of interenterprise arrears in the public sector that may eventually have to be financed by the public budget. These transactions must be specifically recognized in the accounting system so that timely warnings can be sent to policymakers. See Chapter 1.

When payables are explicitly recognized, they must also be taken into consideration in the formulation of budgets. The accumulation of payables implies that liquidity management has become a fiscal policy issue. Normally, liquidity management is viewed as a routine matter, largely concerned with regulating the flow of resources to finance payments. When the fiscal situation is fragile, and limits on domestic credit to the government have been specified (as noted elsewhere, this does not apply to some European countries where central banks have been made independent and no longer provide credit to the government), some countries, engaging in window dressing, have built up payment arrears. In some accounting systems, arrears were not recorded and therefore could not be measured. With the application of computer technology and related software that generates data for each stage of the expenditure process, the measurement of arrears ceased to be a major issue. Indeed, where general ledger systems are in use, the difference between accounts payable at the beginning of the year and at the end of the fiscal year indicates a buildup in payables. To identify purely transitional arrears that reflect delays in the administrative process, the age profile of arrears can easily be gleaned from computer records.

The availability of computer facilities does not necessarily mean that governments will not build up arrears. Indeed, as long as a country's fiscal situation remains fragile, it is only reasonable to assume that the government will avail itself of every policy variable in its arsenal to address what it perceives to be a critical issue. Some policy economists view a buildup in arrears as relatively harmless in that the monetary impact on the economy would be within the limits envisaged at the onset of the fiscal year. This is because the impact is determined by, among other variables, domestic credit, which, in turn, is partly based on the credit expansion that is itself partly based on the credit extended to the government. Such a view ignores a number of other substantive aspects.

First, a buildup in arrears implies that some credit expansion may have already taken place and was recorded, appropriately, as credit to the private sector. In the event, it is the private sector that would be extending informal credit to the government. But no economic agent in the private sector, each one being highly professional and thus rational, would extend such informal credit at the expense of its own profit margin. Indeed, it might be adding more than the expense incurred, its own premium, and therefore would be adding to the overall cost of the services provided by public authorities.

Second, a buildup in arrears may have a more enduring impact on the expenditure control framework. The spending agencies are likely to perceive the buildup as laxity in control and as a leakage that is approved by the central economic ministries. This outcome will be considered a green light to incur more arrears, this time with impunity. This perverse effect is likely to be compounded if the payments process is politicized. When payment arrears accumulate, actual payments are normally made on a first-in, first-out basis. However, when contractors with large pending bills lobby to bring pressure on the paying officials—at the political and civil service levels—the payment queue is likely to be sidestepped, and a political approach for the selection of bills for payment may emerge. This phenomenon has been observed in the past and, given human nature, is likely to continue in the future with attendant costs.

Third, the continued prevalence of arrears in payment implies a steady erosion of the accountability process. Accountability requires that output and income be related in a specific time frame so as to permit proper costing of services. Costing is based on the actual value of goods and services consumed or used in the time frame to provide a given service. Cost-based data would inevitably be different from flow-based data. The discrepancy between those two sets would be heightened in the context of an accumulation of arrears in payment.

It is important that a vigilant eye be kept focused on costing and the accumulation of arrears, so as to anticipate deviations from the approved policies and to ensure that deviations do not become an entrenched part of the expenditure control framework.

Other Funded Liabilities

These transactions refer to the liabilities incurred during an accounting period that are not paid in that period and are thus carried over to the following year. The most common of these liabilities occurs when goods are not immediately available on an off-the-shelf basis and when their supply has long time lags. Some of these lags in delivery may not be recognized by the suppliers, who may have little incentive to expedite delivery once a firm contract is entered into. Although governments are the biggest buyers of goods and services and should enjoy the presumed powers associated with a monopsony, they are often reduced to the level of a Gulliver manipulated by the Lilliputian multitudes of contractors. Although an industrial policy is advocated as a way out of this common experience, the fact remains that in the continuum of the expenditure process, there are several funded liabilities.

Such funding poses some problems, however, in systems where budget appropriations are routinely allowed to lapse. In these cases, the spending agencies are required to persuade the central agencies to continue the allocations in the following year. The central agencies, for their part, may frequently be myopic and view the unspent amounts as savings. In systems that are based on obligation, however, the payment of these liabilities is unlikely to pose any issue as long as proper records are maintained.

Funded liabilities tend to be large in cases where centralized procurement is in place and spending agencies, functioning as clients, draw their supplies from the procurement agency. Previously, transactions among departments were conducted through "suspense" accounts and book adjustments. With the breakup of internal monopolies and with increasing decentralization of procurement responsibilities to spending agencies, this type of funded liability may no longer pose systemic problems.

Contingent Liabilities

These liabilities refer to transactions that arise mostly from guarantees given by governments on behalf of an enterprise owned by it, by a private enterprise, by a nongovernmental organization, or by an individual. Although guarantees existed in one form or another for a number of years, they have become more prevalent since the late 1970s as most of the liabilities stemming from guarantees had to be redeemed by governments. As a result, budget deficits increased. Because many of the guarantees had to be redeemed at short notice during the fiscal year, questions arose as to their nature, the recording of the transactions, recognition during the budgetary process, and related policy action.

A government provides a guarantee when the party concerned does not have the requisite creditworthiness to raise capital or contract a loan on its own and therefore seeks protection under the overall umbrella of the government. To that extent, government intervention undermines market forces, promotes moral hazard and less-than-prudent behavior, and, insofar as the guarantees must be redeemed at a later date, they add to the costs borne by the taxpayer. Guarantees are often provided outside the normal budgetary process after the market has rejected the risk. Initially, this transaction may not attract the attention of the legislature because the liability is not recognized until it falls due, by which time there may be little option but to acquiesce in the transaction and finance the redemption. Although legislatures have recently begun to demand additional information and even prior approval for such transactions, in most countries guarantees are the province of the executive branch, and little organized information is provided to the legislature.

Notwithstanding the well-recognized problems of guarantees and related liabilities, it is unlikely that governments will cease to provide them. Indeed, given that, in general, the public sector is shrinking and the private sector and nongovernmental organizations are providing more services, the use of guarantees may be more extensive than in the past. In response, greater attention must be paid to the formulation of policy packages aimed at addressing these liabilities.

These liabilities can be broadly divided into two categories: formally recognized contingent liabilities and nonquantifiable contingent liabilities. The former are those liabilities that are associated with the provision of guarantees. The latter, considered part of unfunded liabilities, are discussed in the following section. The contingent liabilities are generally recorded only when the contingency is evident, that is, when the guarantee must be redeemed and the necessary budget provision made. The general ledger system used for accounting can also have a subsidiary system devoted to registering and tracking the status of guarantees. As the guarantees become due to be redeemed, the necessary action is initiated to make provisions in the budget. To ensure broader accountability, the government and each agency must prepare an annual statement of contingent liabilities as a part of the overall accounts. These guarantees need to be graded with reference to weights allotted to risks, proportional payment responsibilities (as shareholders), and those that are given to organizations over which governments may not have any control. Thus far, however, experience shows that many countries prepare statements about liabilities but very little information is available on the value of contingent assets. As a result, accounting information is uneven.[3]

By registering and tracking guarantees, the public authorities are able to anticipate future liabilities. If, however, public finances are not to be subjected to short-term stress, it is important that a financing mechanism also be developed. The original objective of a guarantee is to facilitate a third party's receiving a loan but not to subsidize that operation. Because the party seeking the loan is expected to pay the full cost involved, a formula for pricing guarantees is necessary. This raises the larger issue of

---

[3]Considerable attention has been given to guarantees in the United States, and the Federal Accounting Standards Advisory Board has recently developed standards to deal with them.

subsidizing risks. Financial realities have forced some governments, for example in certain Nordic countries, to envisage a pricing formula where part of the guarantee would be redeemed by the government and part through market forces or the private sector. The liability of the government is thereby limited to a specific percentage. This process permits an explicit recognition of this type of liability so as to minimize the shocks on the budget during the course of the fiscal year.

Unfunded Liabilities

In addition to the liabilities described in the preceding sections, several other liabilities need explicit recognition, for example, unfunded liabilities. Some countries have already begun to set up accounting standards that deal with these other liabilities. For example, the financial statements of the Government of New Zealand provide for a recognition of the various types of liabilities described above and also include a listing of nonquantifiable contingent liabilities. Similarly, the agency financial statements prescribed by the Government of the United States (United States, Office of Management and Budget, 1993) include details of liabilities not covered by budgetary resources.

Unfunded liabilities take a variety of forms and, for analytical convenience, may be examined in the following terms: (1) liabilities stemming from legislated guarantees (different from those discussed earlier, which are extended as government policy and at its discretion); (2) liabilities arising from a change in legislation with retrospective effect; (3) hidden liabilities arising from insurance programs; (4) payments arising from the termination of contractual agreements and indemnity payments to compensate contractors for losses incurred in support of government activities; (5) environmental liabilities, such as those arising from the release of hazardous wastes and other pollutants; and (6) payments made to compensate for market failure.

Legislated Guarantees

Any legislation generally includes provisions that make the government responsible for certain types of payments. These may include compensation for disaster victims, liabilities arising from the exercise of official powers, foreign exchange and other losses incurred by the central bank, compensation for third-party claims, payment of taxes and royalties on behalf of government development organizations that have been given a corporate status, liability for previous contracts, assurance of a net rate of return to producers of electricity or fertilizers whose primary buyer and distributor is the government, and provision of foodstuffs to the public at a set price. Out of this vast range, major items, such as subsidies involved in public distribution systems of foodstuffs, are usually estimated and provided for in the budget. The others, largely because of their contingent nature, may not be reflected in the budget. These may come to light long after the requisite legislation has been enacted and, in all probability, are forgotten because of a lack of claims in the interregnum.

Liabilities from Legislative Changes

Experience has shown that a country may enact legislation after the start of the fiscal year to augment existing benefits with retrospective effect as well as to provide new benefits. This represents an unfunded liability. In some cases, awards issued by the judiciary or related adjudication authorities may also have a significant impact on the budget. While some of the awards relating to wage adjustments are anticipated in the form of lump sum appropriations in the budget, those sums may not be adequate and further enhancement may be needed. The judicial awards and legislation with retrospective effect are not usually anticipated because of the uncertainty of the outcome. Such liabilities may be very large and, in the absence of any margin in the budget, would need sudden action that may not be forthcoming.

Hidden Liabilities (3)

In conjunction with providing social safety nets and related benefits, governments have set up separate pension organizations, as well as pension benefit guarantees when pensions are organized by employer organizations. In the former case, benefits are paid out on a pay-as-you-go basis. When the annual benefits are substantially higher than contributions, the difference is funded by a transfer from the government budget. When the government budget itself is running a deficit, the pension organizations in some countries are encouraged ostensibly as a short-term approach (but which often becomes a continuing practice) to borrow funds from the public. The annual budgets of both the government and the pension organization may not fully reveal actual practices and thus would not show the hidden liabilities.[4]

In some instances (for example, the Pension Benefit Guarantee Corporation in the United States), employee retirement funds are insured by a corporation set up by the government. These employee funds may not be fully funded, and funding may depend on the prevailing tax legislation. In Japan, for example, companies provide up to the maximum tax-allowable amount—usually 50 percent of the amount payable if employees ceased employment at balance sheet date.[5] To that extent, the accounts would understate the liability for pensions. When such pension plans are insured by the government corporation and when the plans terminate with insufficient assets to cover their benefit obligations, the corporation assumes the liability for the funding of benefits. The corporation then values the assets it receives and the liabilities it is responsible for financing. Usually, however, the assets are not adequate (given the moral hazard situations associated with insurance activity), and the overall difference constitutes a hidden liability and therefore a hidden or informal debt of the government.[6] Similar instances may be found in other industrial and developing countries. Experience also shows that, in the absence of adequate accounting and proper liability tracking, sudden fiscal crises may emerge with a lasting impact on governments' financial plans.

Termination of Contracts

In some special circumstances, firm contracts that have been legally entered into by governments may be revoked for, among other reasons,

---

[4]Specifically in regard to pensions, there is in general an implicit public debt. A recent report by the World Bank (1994b, p. 90) observes that, because of its emphasis on current cash payments, pay-as-you-go finance hides the true long-run costs of pension promises. The current situation is only the tip of the iceberg. When workers pay their social security taxes, they expect to get a specific benefit in return. The present value of this future stream of expected benefits is known as the "implicit public pension debt." This liability for the government, corresponding to the "entitlement" people believe they have acquired, is the iceberg underneath the tip. Although this implicit debt varies by country and depends on the coverage of the pension system, the age distribution of workers, the level of benefits, and the discount rate used in the calculation, in many countries, *it is two or three times the value of the conventional explicit debt* (emphasis added). To some extent, this is abetted by government budget practices. Budgets usually based on cash are limited to a fiscal year and to that extent do not recognize hidden debt. If hidden debt is recognized, budgets do not reveal its magnitude.

[5]For a comparative survey of three practices, see International Capital Markets Group (1992).

[6]For an illustrative discussion of these aspects, see United States, General Accounting Office (1989 and 1992b).

a lack of funding. Termination frequently involves payment for violation of contractual agreements. Payment may be voluntary or made through awards arrived at through a judicial or quasi-judicial process. Termination of contracts, while not unusual, may occur more frequently in the future. As services are contracted out, or as international bidding (to be monitored by the proposed World Trade Organization) becomes obligatory, contracts are likely to become more complex. Inevitably, the judicial process will be invoked more frequently than it has been in the past.

Environmental Liabilities

Public consciousness about the impact of pollution has risen and is likely to rise further as greater investments are made in the production of basic chemicals and related industries. Governments in both industrial and developing countries have enacted legislation for the treatment of industrial wastes. In some countries, current legislation stipulates that industries should also limit the disposal and treatment of waste. While legislation may be adequate, or may need selective strengthening, the more important fact is that waste control technology is not fully secure.[7] When leakages occur, the potential for third-party liabilities increases. These liabilities, which are difficult to anticipate and estimate, must be borne by the government. In addition, extreme cases of leakage occasionally occur, such as those in Bhopal, India and in Chernobyl, where some relief expenditure had to be incurred from the public exchequer.

Market Failure Liabilities

The public authorities may be required to step in, even when insurance provision exists, to correct major market failures. A typical instance is the failure of commercial banking institutions, where the deposit insurance funds may not be adequate and the assets of the institutions are far from marketable. In these cases, maintaining public confidence and market stability is of paramount importance, and governments may have no

---

[7]For a discussion of the experience of the United States, see General Accounting Office (1990b). The GAO later recommended that the insurance companies engaged in property and casualty insurance should disclose annually the number and type of environmental claims and the estimated range of associated claim costs and expenses. See also United States, General Accounting Office (1993).

short-term option other than to intervene and shift the burden to the tax-payers. The losses of a few would be offset by the contributions of the many. Estimating these liabilities would be like estimating the size of the iceberg from its tip and is therefore problematic.

The preceding scenarios illustrate the likelihood of the annual fiscal policy stance receiving shocks from a variety of sources. What should a government do? It is a truism that in governmental activities, as in other human activities, what needs to be addressed must be properly measured; what needs to be measured must be identified and defined. Decision makers cannot be soothsayers, but their consideration and judgment are made easier when their tasks are defined and measured properly. The government accounting system needs to be designed so as to provide opportunities for the agencies to record the type of liabilities described above.

The commercial-type accounts introduced in Australia, New Zealand, and the United States provide, with varying coverage, for the recording of these liabilities. Simply recording the transactions is not a solution. The role of recording is to disclose the financial condition of the entity and the government and the liabilities that need to be explicitly recognized as part of the annual budget exercise. The size of the liabilities may be larger than estimated and may tend to mushroom after the start of the fiscal year. As Benjamin Disraeli once noted, "what we anticipate seldom occurs; what we least expect generally happens." For this reason, the accounting information on liabilities must be functionally integrated with the annual budget process to provide a basis for scenario planning for policymakers. Such efforts may not offer full protection, but, by improving preparedness, they imply a radical departure from the old order of managing the crisis when it actually occurs.

A related approach is to create an unallocated budgetary reserve to meet contingent situations. Experience, however, shows that every reserve, regardless of its specific and legitimate objectives, attracts a lot of claimants and the use of the reserves would become a contentious and highly politicized issue. Moreover, when the overall fiscal stance is tight, there would be little leeway to allocate separate resources for reserves. It is more prudent to have systems that permit the recording and tracking of these liabilities so that they may be appropriately addressed. In the absence of such systems, the results would be (and have been) different, reminding policymakers of Anthony Eden's words (1960, p. 520): "It is impossible to read the record now and not feel that we had a responsibility for always being a lap behind—always a lap behind, the fatal lap."

Debt Management

Before development planning was the norm, the debt of most countries, except during such emergencies as wars, was small and manageable. For the most part, such debt was raised on behalf of the government by the central bank in its capacity as the government's fiscal agent. The day-to-day management of the debt was also generally handled by the central bank. Because many countries did not have a developed capital market, the issues were also subscribed, in large measure, by the central bank. In addition, the central bank provided advances to the government for ways and means and related overdrafts. For all intents and purposes, the central bank and the government had an intimate relationship. Any debt raised by the central bank was redeemed through regular budgetary appropriations, and in several cases governments maintained a wide variety of sinking funds as a manifestation of their financial prudence and overall trustworthiness. In retrospect, such an effort appears misplaced in a context where there were no organized capital markets.

In due course, arrangements were made for each type of issue of public debt, with fairly simple accounting conventions. Broadly, three types of transactions were recognized. First, there were specific fund liabilities, which were directly related to and expected to be paid from proprietary and trust funds. These liabilities were limited to the specific funds. Second, there was the long-term debt, which was secured more through the government's general credit and revenue-raising powers than through its sinking funds. Third, debt was issued, mostly at the local level in industrial countries, to finance capital projects. Each project was funded by a separate issue of debt and was expected to be paid from the revenues raised after the project became fully operational. The accounting system was accrual-based in that a liability was registered as soon as it became apparent. This was a common feature even in those systems that were traditionally considered to be cash-based ones.

Developments

This picture of accounting changed radically during the early 1950s when debt financing came to be viewed as an instrument in the government's regular financing arsenal. During the 1970s and 1980s, both the domestic debt and the external debt increased substantially. Meanwhile, it was found that maintaining sinking funds was no longer appropriate in a context where debt was extinguished through new issues of debt rather than from accumulated reserves. As the external debt grew, it became necessary to pay more attention to institutional and accounting issues. A number of countries, mostly at the instance of international financial institutions, set up computer-operated external debt recording and monitoring systems.[8]

The exponential growth in debt has rapidly transformed the way in which debt is managed, the way monitorable limits on the levels of debt are established, and a government's relationship with its central bank. There are major differences in the way industrial countries and developing countries organize debt, but the differences are shrinking with the opening of economies and the associated globalization of trade. In the industrial countries, several new instruments for borrowing in domestic and external markets have been introduced. Other developments include an intensified internalization of government securities markets, an improvement in the depth and liquidity of wholesale markets for government securities, and the increased availability of improved market functioning and market management through "specialists in government securities (primary dealers)." Associated with this growing market diversification, there was greater automation in the securities market and more efficient clearing and settlement procedures.[9]

The alarming increase in debt and its impact on countries' fiscal health has induced governments to pursue policies aimed at reducing the growth of debt. One of the principal aims of fiscal policy in many European countries during the 1980s was to contain the deficit so that the debt, too, could be limited. In addition to policy measures, this stance also took the form of legislating, through constitutional amendment, the size of the deficit and the limits on borrowing. In the Western European countries, these efforts culminated in the Maastricht Treaty, which specified acceptable levels for the deficit and the outstanding debt. While the operational aspects remain to be fully worked out, these specifications have become a restraining influence on the member countries and have induced them to undertake more urgent measures aimed at fiscal consolidation. In sum, the treaty puts a stop to the practices of recent years of incurring burgeoning deficits and financing them through internal and external borrowing. Hereafter, the governments are expected to be

---

[8]Separate off-the-shelf software was provided by the Commonwealth Secretariat, United Nations Conference on Trade and Development, and the World Bank. These efforts have facilitated the central dissemination of information on external debt by the IMF and the World Bank.

[9]For a detailed discussion see Broker (1993), pp. 15–19.

bound by the Maastricht conventions. These developments could have an emulating effect on other countries.

In early 1994, member countries of the European Union began to enact legislation to make their central banks independent of the government. Hereafter, central banks would no longer provide short-term advances. In fact, they would not participate in the primary market of government securities. Increasingly, governments would be looking into the prospect of regulating the depth and liquidity of wholesale markets for government securities. These trends are likely to promote similar practices in other countries, including in the developing world.

The complex new environment in which public debt management will be undertaken has several elements, of which accounting is only one. But accounting must adapt to the context in which it is expected to work and must internalize the changes in its day-to-day operations. The accounting manager is not a substitute for a debt portfolio manager, neither of whom can function without the other. Indeed, the portfolio manager has a unique dependence on the accountant. Accountants and related professionals must recognize and reorient themselves to the changing world.

Continuing Objectives

In reorienting accounting traditions, due note should also be taken of the principles, or objectives, of debt management policy. Here again, there is a marked difference between the monetary policy orientation of the portfolio manager and the orientation of the accountant. The former is more concerned with the market impact of the proposed issue of debt, the choice of instruments, and the interest rate, as well as the maturity profile of the issue. The accountant is likely to be more concerned, by virtue of his or her assigned functions, with the structuring of assets to match liabilities. As governments compete more among themselves and with the private sector, accountants are expected to function more like comptrollers in the commercial world managing their assets, so that, in the eyes of the public, net worth is preserved or increased. Accountants perform in the open and under the vigilant eye of the public and cannot resort to sleight of hand.

Matching assets and liabilities is a formidable and complex task. In governments, there is more information and certainty about liabilities than about assets. The normal assets on which information is available are liquid assets, such as cash balances and foreign exchange reserves (including gold), and, to a lesser extent, the investment portfolio (the financial shares held) and recoverable loans. The valuation of these assets, however, is likely to be subject to volatility, reflecting changes in the interest rate and exchange rates. Physical assets, as reflected in the national income accounts, show the strength and the potential of the economy rather than the net worth. A compilation of assets would throw light on a country's net worth and the degree of openness of the government. A distinction must be drawn between foreign and domestic liabilities, so that matching assets can be arranged. Although the overall task is much larger than may be performed by accountants alone, they play an important role.

One objective common to the accountant and the debt manager relates to borrowing costs. As borrowing becomes a regular feature of the management of government finances, the need for containing costs becomes paramount. This consideration did not previously dominate government financial management because the central bank generally managed most day-to-day debt operations. With increasing independence for the central banks, debt management is likely to revert to the governments. Cost containment in the management of debt has two elements. The first involves securing the best possible terms for the proposed issue and finding a method that is both administratively simpler and cheaper. The second relates to the administrative costs of the organization engaged in the management of the debt.

Securing the best possible terms is an overriding objective for both the accountant and the portfolio manager. Their roles may get so intermingled in the process that it is hard to determine where the accountant's role stops and the manager's starts. (It could in fact be argued that these distinctions are artificial and that they do not, in practice, exist. The distinctions are helpful, however, in clarifying their roles.) This strong relationship becomes even stronger in a context where the instruments and their costs and risks are constantly changing. The issue of debt in several countries is managed in close consultation with banks and other financial institutions, which generally receive fees for their services. In some cases, the fees are substantial and contribute to the higher costs of borrowing. Such increases in costs may have their own dynamics and may partly nullify the strenuous efforts made to contain the costs incurred in the provision of goods and services. Alternatives such as auctions, which generally do not involve the payment of fees and commissions, may have to be explored. These efforts must go hand in hand with efforts to contain organizational costs (see discussion below).

Organization

Debt management, which is relatively simple and structured, falls into four broad categories of administrative arrangements. (1) In general, the issue and day-to-day management of debt are handled by the central bank. (2) In some countries, the management of external debt is handled by the finance or planning ministry (in conjunction with foreign aid), and domestic aid issues are handled by the central bank.[10] (3) In some cases, both foreign and domestic debt are under the jurisdiction of the government, although the central bank, acting as fiscal agent of the government, may be maintaining the debt register—that is, holding debt. (4) In a few cases, the national debt, comprising both external and domestic debt, may be administered by a separate organization that is directly accountable to the legislature or organized as a separate or autonomous fund within the overall guidance of the government.[11]

Although these relationships have generally been designed for administrative convenience or the financial credibility of governments, they need to be reviewed with reference to three criteria. First, do these arrangements have the effect of reducing the independent role the central bank is expected to perform? As debt instruments become more diversified and greater reliance is placed on primary markets for sustaining the debt issues, it may be administratively convenient to shift to the government some of the burdens currently assumed by the central bank. Such an arrangement, while providing the requisite independence to the bank, may also make the government's fiscal behavior more responsible and prudent. This shift also implies that governments can borrow on their own creditworthiness. Second, given the inherent close linkages between debt and fiscal and monetary policies, the administration should be so located as to serve the immediate needs of both. In principle, organizational fragmentation can be offset by a technology-driven information system, which makes information available to all participants at the same time. There may, however, be some advantage in locating the center of administration closer to the action—that is, to the ministries of finance. And, third, the costs of each arrangement should be explicitly evaluated with reference to the advantages and disadvantages of each.

---

[10]Even in this context there may be different arrangements. In some countries, treasury bills, usually of a duration of 90 days, are issued by the ministries of finance, while securities of other types are managed by the central banks.

[11]Some autonomous funds were set up during the interwar years in France at a time when the financial credibility of the government was very low. This later became a common feature in French-type accounting systems.

Role of Accounting

The first contribution of an accounting system to the management of debt is its ability to determine the borrowing requirement. The difference between receipts and expected outlays is the usual basis for determining the overall borrowing requirement. However, the entire amount so determined may not be borrowed from the public, primarily because the government manages several funds in a trust capacity, including provident funds, pension funds, and other deposits. Most of them are expected, either by law or by convention (which by force of habit may have the same applicability as law), to be invested in government securities.[12] In addition, most foreign borrowing, including from international financial institutions, may represent parts of an ongoing program rather than totally new borrowing. These amounts are also estimated by the accounting system. In addition, through their effort to restructure the external debt, governments have also been engaged in debt-for-equity and debt-for-debt swaps.[13] In all stages of determining the overall magnitude of government debt, as well as the choice of bargaining strategies to renegotiate the debt, accounting plays a prominent role.

In these and related areas, the preferred basis of accounting is accrual. A cash-based system would be inadequate to indicate the full ramifications of the debt. An accrual system is therefore conventionally used to register short- and long-term liabilities and the process for liquidating them. Curiously, the systems in practice follow the accrual approach only for public debt transactions and not for registering the wide variety of unfunded and contingent liabilities discussed earlier in this chapter. One option is to maintain an accrual-based accounting system with appropriate bridges to the cash system. The accrual principle as now implemented by many governments is rather rudimentary. Ideally, for example, under the accrual system all costs would be allocated to the period in

---

[12]This could mean that those funds are earning less than they would have secured if they had been invested in private securities. To that extent, they subsidize the government by reducing their debt-servicing burden. But the extent of this subsidization cannot be ascertained with precision, as the accounting systems are not structured to calculate these amounts.

[13] In a debt-for-equity swap, foreign commercial banks are given local currency for their foreign-denominated debt, which they can then invest in a local project. Governments usually set limits on eligible projects and the repatriation of dividends and principal.

Under the debt-for-debt program, the foreign commercial bank exchanges government debt for a debt owed to the government by a private or government-owned corporation. The corporation then undergoes a capital restructuring so that the debt becomes common equity. There have also been cases of debt-for-environmental-improvement swaps. As a part of this swap, international wildlife preservation funds are channeled to selected developing countries experiencing depleting ecologies.

which they are incurred and to the instrument from which they originate. Thus, interest costs would be spread over the life of the security rather than being shown as an expense item (as in the cash-based system) in the year in which it is redeemed.[14]

It is also necessary, in the interest of accountability, that the costs involved (including fees and the value of a number of tax incentives, such as the postal savings certificates) be calculated so that the costs of government policy preferences can be established. As an extension of this, it is necessary to show all debt instruments at their current market value, including both gains and losses. This would allow debt managers to wind up or withdraw some instruments whose coupon rate of interest is below par and, thus, whose redemption costs would be substantially reduced. Both criteria suggest that the accrual principle should be carried to its logical conclusion and that a balance sheet statement and income and expenditure statement cf debt should be prepared. These statements would show how governments are managing their vast public debt, costs incurred (including opportunities lost), and gains made.

When the public debt is substantial, cash management in government is likely to be affected in more than one way. For example, bunching of interest and debt repayments could skew the pattern of spending, and considerable borrowing may be required at certain times of the year. If a borrowing episode were to coincide with the busy season of the year insofar as credit markets are concerned, the costs of borrowing may be higher than anticipated. For this reason, the accounting system has the responsibility of indicating, at the onset of the fiscal year, the timing involved in debt-payment operations. These links will be well serviced when the debt system is computerized and detailed information is available on payments due, so that the central budget managers can take them into account in formulating their cash management plans for an entire year.

The accounting system also has a major role in maintaining the public debt register and an efficient system to pay debt holders. The first function involves printing, maintaining, and delivering physical certificates representing the debt titles. In a number of countries, more often in the developing world, a long lag is observed between the subscription to the

---

[14]This has an impact on the size of the budget deficit. In estimating budget deficits, repayments are netted against new loans and the net estimates are shown, for analytical purposes, as a below-the-line item. The detailed transactions may be shown in the budgets even when such outlays are considered as *charged* or requiring no legislative approval.

Where, however, debt instruments are issued at zero-coupon rates, interest costs would be included in budget estimates only at the time of their redemption. Meanwhile, the budget deficit would appear lower, although in reality it is growing all the time.

debt issue and the supply of the physical certificates. The lag occurs primarily because the entries are made manually in the register and could, in turn, contribute to a situation where financial derivatives introduce a good deal of speculative activity into the equation.[15] This has the potential of working against the stated objectives of monetary policy.

The payment process includes reconciliation between the debt register and the actual payments. Governments or their central banks maintain individual accounts of the holders of public debt so that necessary authorization can be issued for the payment of interest and principal. But because the actual payments may be made by another agency, discrepancies may emerge between the register and the payments. For this reason, a regular reconciliation between the two is essential.[16] Payments to debt holders may, depending on how the accounting system is organized, involve two stages: authorization from the government account, and from the central bank or commercial banks designated for the purpose to the holders of the debt. While it is natural to expect these two stages to be synchronized, in practice administrative delays at both ends have made debt holders cynical. In some countries, the payment function has been transferred to commercial banks, particularly where the transactions are large and frequent.

The complexity of government operations is clearly growing, giving rise to a need to review accounting systems and ways to strengthen them. These issues will become more important in the future as operations become even more complex. The need for early action cannot be overemphasized.

---

[15]This was experienced in India during 1993. Scheduled banks started exchanging scrips and providing advances on the basis of the prospective delivery of debt certificates. The speculative activity, as a result, was substantial.

[16]This was one of the problems experienced in the administration of debt in the United States. See General Accounting Office (1990c).

5

Architecture of Government Financial Information

Writing about financial reporting could easily mean writing about the lack of information on the financial status of the government. There is a general impression that, notwithstanding periodic pronouncements about transparency and the availability of information about the financial implications of proposed or ongoing policies, there is very little organized information. What is provided is frequently incomplete, incomprehensible, or out of date. The purpose of this chapter is not to authenticate this impression, but to accept as a starting point that, in most countries financial reporting originated in the enactment of the budget law a long time ago. Since then, the needs of the government and the public have become more varied and complex. While governments have made gradual efforts to meet some of the growing demands, they do not appear to have kept up, and not all demands have been adequately addressed.

Less than a decade ago, heads of the audit offices in two industrial countries noted: "In spite of the real interest in government financial reporting, *there has been no consensus* [emphasis added] on what information federal governments should record and report. Many hypotheses have been put forward but, until recently, there has been little organized effort to reconcile conflicting views and obtain a consensus. The time now seems most appropriate for such an effort."[1] Indeed, there seems to be greater agreement now on what is needed, when it is needed, and how it may be furnished.

Importance of Financial Information

Traditionally in countries where legislatures played an important role in considering and approving fiscal policies and controlling appropria-

---

[1]See United States, General Accounting Office and Canada, Office of the Auditor General (1986), pp. 3–4.

tions of money, the government was legally bound to report periodically on the progress achieved in budget implementation. Later, as a part of the concluding activity of the budget cycle, governments were also required to submit accounts to the legislature and an audit agency. This legal tradition, which prevails in many countries, also provided the framework for accounting practices. Accounts were submitted in terms of the original appropriations so that any variations and their sources could be examined.

This practice of legislative accountability was not a feature of the administrative systems of the former centrally planned economies, which had no formal procedure for reviewing the budget or the accounts for the previous year. The emphasis in these countries was on inspections rather than on post audits. Under central planning, accounting systems distinguished between the statistical record specified by the planning agencies and the financial record needed for financial management. Since every step of an activity was accounted for in the plan, progress had to be reported back to the central agencies. This tradition of reporting emphasized the internal management needs of the central and spending agencies and the government as a whole. These two elements, namely, legislative accountability and financial reporting for internal management, now form the twin parameters of financial information systems. The systems have acquired a new urgency in the context of recent political, social, and economic developments.

Politically, the most important development to affect reporting has been the increase in the number of democracies. As countries move from dictatorships to democracies, where the legislature plays a decisive role, there is also a growth in the demand for accountability, for transparent decision making, and for rule of law. These demands, when applied to financial management, translate into additional information that will shed light both on how decisions are reached by the executive and on how they are implemented. Furthermore, recent changes in established democracies—such as the United Kingdom—which have been seeking a greater role for citizen participation, have also contributed to additional demands for financial information.

Finally, the growth of satellite technology has narrowed the gap between the government and its citizens, and each is seeking to influence the other on social choices. It is now suggested that the state has moved from theater to television orientation and that a few minutes on television could have a greater impact than demonstrations by half a million people. The government for its part would prefer to provide more information about its strong point—that is, providing public services. The citizens seek both additional services as well as changes in the quality of the services provided. Each party seeks feedback from the other. Both positions emphasize the need for regular and unbiased information so that the debate can be both objective and informed.

Developments in the social sector represent changes in the composition of public expenditures. Since the late 1980s, a greater share of government expenditures has been devoted to social transfers, including pensions, safety nets, and poverty alleviation measures. In the process, governments have initiated several social welfare measures that have generated intense debates about the benefits of these expenditures and how the benefits may be improved. The information provided by governments is greatly influenced by the social and political context in which information is sought and provided. The key to greater public awareness and improved citizen participation is information. But information is a double-edged sword. It may favor the cause of the providers or, if the performance is less desirable than expected, it could and often does backfire on the provider of information. Despite such risks, the provider cannot suppress information that may portray it in a negative light. It is the obligation of governments to make information available to society.

Economic developments emphasize the contextual nature of some demands for financial information by the government. The traditional demand, which is embodied in the practices of most governments, is to provide accounts showing how public money is spent. This demand is now supplemented by other demands for periodic information on how economic policy instruments are being used and how successful they are. Many governments now have mandatory ceilings on the total level of expenditures, on the size of the deficit, and on outlays on specific programs, such as defense and entitlements. When the government exceeds these ceilings, procedures for sequestering funds may be invoked. The use of such instruments of control suggests that those both inside and outside government need regular information about government operations.

Public and Private Sectors Compared

The features described above suggest that governments have become, by accident, by design, or through an evolutionary process, veritable glass houses, with much of their decision making taking place in the public eye. This feature, among others, distinguishes it from the private sector, although the two sectors share several features in common, and it is useful to compare the two systems.

Both private and public sectors are accountable for their actions. Both are funded by the public, the former somewhat more selectively, and the latter with greater public participation. Both offer services to the public—the private sector at a price that includes remuneration for the capital employed. The government may or may not charge for the services it offers. Both raise capital, but the government has the coercive power to levy taxes to finance the provision of services. Both incur short- and medium-term liabilities. Both are accountable for funds raised and for charges levied.

In contrast, the two sectors traditionally use different accounting frameworks. The commercial organization submits to its board a budget, which, owing to competitive rivalry, may never be published and, at the end of the accounting period, submits a balance sheet and associated income and expenditure statements. In the private sector, the balance sheet has a bottom line, that is, profits or losses made. Moreover, its performance may be appraised more objectively and systematically because other enterprises exist that are engaged in similar activities.

In contrast, the government's actions are more open. In most cases, the government budget is a public document that undergoes changes, usually between initial submission by the executive and final approval by the legislature. The government also submits its accounts at the end of the fiscal year. Government provides a vast array of services, some of which are not provided by any other organization. Its uniqueness makes comparison difficult, and performance appraisal has the potential of being contentious. Because, in government, the profit motive coexists with the provision of services for only a few activities, its accounts have not aimed at providing information on overall assets and liabilities, much less on future liabilities that need additional financing. Over the years, governments have sought to analyze these aspects through forward budgets, comprehensive national income accounts that provide data on stocks and flows, and other supplementary sources of information.

The dissimilarities between the public and private sectors have given rise to suggestions that commercial-type accounting formats be applied to governments. The rest of this chapter considers, among other issues, the traditional architecture of information in governments and how it addresses the users' concerns. Two additional features of government operations should be noted. The unique features of government services are not fully captured in normal budgets or related accounts, which usually show the common inputs (manpower, money, and materials) and their use. For this reason, patterns in the use of inputs may not present comparable pictures of services provided. It may also be difficult to establish a precise relationship between the resources governments raise and the services they provide. Second, the design of government information systems, as will be illustrated throughout the chapter, may reflect more the exercise of internal controls than the needs of the users. Information tends to be viewed as a natural product of government financial management rather than as a product designed to meet the needs of outsiders. This latter feature, which is influenced by, among other things, shareholders' rights for disclosure and concerns for investors' protection, is common to the commercial world too.

Principles of Reporting

Reports prepared by the government for internal and external use are tacitly governed by eight principles, which are described below.

Legitimacy

The term "financial statement" is generic and is likely to have different meanings for different groups. Reports should be appropriate for the intended users and prepared according to specific standards for their form and content. The specification of standards implies a mutual understanding between the user and the provider on the nature and content of financial information and does not necessarily require either a decree, an executive order, or legislation. Rather, convention may serve this function.

Understandability

The broad purpose of financial reports is to provide accountability. To be "accountable," according to the dictionary, is to be "obliged to explain one's actions, to justify what one does." Accordingly, the reports should be understandable to the user. But because there is no one typical user with defined and immutable characteristics, this principle should be primarily viewed as an exhortation to be clear and simple. The important question is: What changes are needed in the presentation of financial reports to be of service to the prospective user? In the process of making these changes, a determination needs to be made to avoid manipulating inherently complex information, because attempts to simplify it may rob it of its significance.[2]

Reliability

Financial reports are expected to be objective. As noted earlier, organizations in the public and private sectors would like, indeed expect, the information to serve their needs. This can be considered a necessary ingredient of the organizational rationality. The characteristics of reliable information are somewhat difficult to enumerate and explain. But those that would nullify the intent of the reports are easier to identify. First, facts must be distinguished from estimates. Although, as a discipline, accounting necessarily implies the verification of facts, some reports may contain information derived from estimates. In the mind of the user, the degree of estimation determines the reliability of the data. The methodology of estimation should therefore be explained, and, as the methodology changes, the differences (and the different results likely to accrue) should also be explained. In some cases, the coverage of the data will determine the conclusions that may be drawn from the reports. Here again, the user would prefer to be informed at the outset of any changes made. Reliability does not mean consistency for its own sake. It is more important that users be fully informed about changes than that they be obliged to discover changes on their own, which can only breed cynicism.

Relevance

Information is provided in response to an explicitly recognized need. Thus, the traditional role of providing accounts for the completed fiscal year was to inform the legislature about what had happened during that period. This feature implies the need to identify the users and their

---

[2]Suggestions have been made from time to time about how financial information reports should be made user friendly. Likierman suggests, for example, that the report should "(a) minimize jargon and acronyms and not be patronizing, (b) have a logical structure and layout, (c) have a summary of key points, (d) not have an overwhelming amount of detail, (e) not be unduly distorted by public relations considerations, (f) be clear about the nature, cost, and progress of major projects, and (g) be clear about the impact of changing price levels." He adds that there should be a good balance between figures, text, and charts and clear textual explanation of figures. See Likierman (1989), p. 29.

requirements. One common criticism of government financial information is that there is a surfeit, not a shortage. Many accounts are prepared and provided without taking into account the users' needs. Indeed, some say that much information is produced routinely, on the basis of tradition rather than of need. Over time, some information may become irrelevant; meanwhile, the provision of information continues unchanged. Relevance cannot be assumed. Users must be purposefully identified and distinguished by type and by interest.

Comparability

Rendering accountability means that an organization is willing to submit itself to evaluation—a complex process that involves several steps, one of which is to compare like activities. The data reported should provide a frame of reference for comparing organizations with similar functions so that the costs of providing similar services can be estimated. This process assumes major political and economic significance at the subnational level within a country and when a country is a member of a regional organization. The devolution of common resources can involve assessing the relative efforts made to ensure economy and efficiency in expenditure. The provision of comparable data can also involve rearranging data to conform with the classification selected. Thus, annual accounts, which are generally arranged in terms of appropriation categories, would need to be reclassified. Providing comparable data is yet another manifestation of being responsive to user needs.

Timeliness

The processes of the judiciary and the information provision machinery have a common feature. For both, delay can invalidate their existence. If information is supplied long after the event for which it is intended, the message to users is that compliance is perfunctory. In most governments, however (and also sometimes in the commercial world), accounting data are not released until they are approved or cleared by the audit agency (or in the case of a company, by the board of directors). Delays that represent organizational slippages may occur even when information is intended for internal government use. Sometimes, information is delayed because it is not made available until it has been found to comply fully with the law. In other cases, delays may result from undue efforts to be precise. Although a lack of precision may affect reliability, there is an inevitable trade-off between precision and timeliness. For the sake of timeliness, some precision may have to be sacrificed.

Consistency

The reports should be consistent over time in terms of coverage (nature of the entity reporting), classification, and the accounting basis. Consistency does not mean rejection of needed and feasible improvements as long as the rationale for the changes is clear. Consistency facilitates the preparation and use of data and leads to a mutually acceptable framework.

Usefulness

The final criterion for financial reporting is usefulness. To be useful both inside and outside an agency, reports should contribute to an understanding of the current and future activities of the agency's sources and uses of funds and the diligence shown in the use of funds.

The above principles, which are unexceptional and universal, are applicable to both financial and nonfinancial data, such as performance measures. If the principles are considered universal, why then does practice diverge from precept? The answer is found in the fact that information is an instrument of management. Like other instruments, it can be both used and abused.

Existing Information Systems

Notwithstanding the limitations of generalizations and variations in country practices, some broad statements may be made about the financial information produced by government. First, governments generate vast amounts of financial information. A list of illustrative documents and the type of information generated is shown in Table 11. Second, to a large extent, the origins of the documents and their availability to the public are governed by relevant laws, specific rules, or convention. For example, reports on a country's macroeconomic situation are published by the central bank as a service to the community to facilitate informed debate about the content of proposed policies. Annual accounts are

Table 11. A Typical Reporting System

Description	Distribution	Features
General economic and fiscal situation		
Report on the macroeconomic situation	Internal document.	Prepared by the ministry of finance for internal monitoring purposes.
Report on the economic situation	Internal document.	Prepared by the central bank for use by the government.
Government finances		
Annual budget	This is a public document in most countries. In some, however, it is viewed as a confidential document and not available to the public.	Sets out the details of revenues, expenditures, and debt. Is mostly intended for parliamentary legislation.
Mid-term budget or review	Same as above.	Same as above.
Monthly report on revenues, expenditures, and services of finance	In some countries, this is an internal document. In others, it is a public document and is also published in the central bank bulletin.	Provides summary as well as details of each component. Public enterprise operations are not generally included.
Weekly report on government finances	Intended for internal use in the governments.	Contains the broad aggregates.
Daily report on government finances	Same as above.	This report is usually based on the aggregates furnished by the banking system at the end of each working day on the transactions made and on the status of balances.
Annual accounts	Generally available to the public. They are intended in most cases for legislative approval and related action. In some countries these are intended for internal use only.	These are compiled by the accountant general for submission to the audit institution and to the parliament.
Annual audit report	Produced in almost all countries where supreme audit institutions function. These annual reports are published and are available for public use.	The report contains, in most cases, detailed review of the appropriation accounts and the issues awaiting legislative enquiry and action.
Revenues		
Weekly reports on revenue collected	Mostly internal use.	The reports show the collections under each category of revenue.
Monthly reports on revenue collected	Same as above. As noted earlier, summary of revenues collected may be published.	Same as above.

Expenditures		
Weekly statement of expenditures	Internal use.	These are compiled by the spending or central agencies and show the progress in expenditure under each category.
Monthly report on expenditures	As noted above, this is generally published.	These statements show the details of expenditures for each department and agency.
Cash status		
Cash receipts and expenditures	Internal use.	As noted above, daily information on the aggregates is prepared on the basis of "control totals" conveyed by the banking system.
Other categories		
Status of nonbudget funds	Internal use.	Prepared on an ad hoc basis for internal use.
Foreign aid	This is part of published information—annually, in many countries.	Amounts of aid promised, delivered, and utilized are shown.
Domestic debt	Generally published by the central bank through weekly press releases or monthly bulletins.	Details of outstanding debt, new issues, and movements in debt are provided.
Foreign debt	More frequent reports (weekly, monthly) are published for internal use. For the public, information is available on an annual basis.	Reports show the outstanding debt, its features, maturity pattern, and projects financed.
Performance data on the activities of the agencies	In a few countries, departments publish performance data in their annual reports.	Annual reports, when produced, provide a good deal of detail on agencies' activities.
Future budgets	In a few countries, both recurrent and investment budgets show future needs.	The extent of detail varies. In general, the program and project outlays show future needs.
State enterprises	Consolidated information on the enterprise sector is available in only a few countries. In some, enterprises publish their annual balance sheets but these are not consolidated.	Where consolidated data are available, they provide detailed accounts in terms of balance sheets, income and expenditure statements, and statements on the sources and use of funds.
Local finances	Consolidated information of central and local finances is available in very few countries. In some countries there is a selective consolidation of selected local governments.	This consolidation, which is usually undertaken by independent organizations, or the central banks, seeks to provide financial data for each level of government.

generally required by law to be submitted to the legislature. Several government economic organizations have, over time, undertaken the preparation of reports on specific aspects of public finances. For example, revenue services publish data on sources of revenue, while others compile data on foreign debt for management purposes. A natural consequence of this process is that the information generated reflects the territorial interests of that organization. This in turn leads to differences in the orientation and disaggregation of the data generated.

The third generalization is that the information generated is intended primarily for internal use, partly because data are confidential but also because government information systems were originally designed for internal use. Finally, the reporting system has evolved over the years. Increasingly, as budgets have developed, in some countries, a vast amount of information on the status of government finances is provided to the legislature and the public. Moreover, the frequency of budgets has increased (particularly in high-inflation countries) and, in some countries, mid-term budgetary reviews have become obligatory and are required to be submitted to the legislature.

Search for User Needs

Despite its availability, information needs to be made more purposeful to enhance its usefulness. This need is perceived differently by the providers of information on the one hand, and by the users on the other hand. The former suggest that the reports remain, for the most part, unread. Likierman (1989) states that minimal response and low sales of the reports justify this view. He adds that "it is often difficult for compilers to understand that few people even know that their reports exist" at all (p. 29). The users, on the other hand, appear to feel that the data need to be better organized in explicit recognition of their needs. But then, who are the users and what are their needs? Admittedly, users and their purposes in seeking financial information differ from time to time, from place to place, and according to context. To identify users, audit agencies in Canada and the United States conducted a survey in 1986,[3] yielding revealing results. The survey divided users into six broad categories—legislators and citizens; media and special interest groups; government planners and managers; economists; corporate users; and lenders and se-

---

[3]See United States, General Accounting Office, and Canada, Office of the Auditor General (1986).

curities dealers.[4] The results of the survey are summarized in Table 12. The responses suggest that except for specific items, such as reporting on pension liabilities, gold holdings of the government, accrual of tax revenues, asset valuation, and performance indicators, there is considerable commonality of interests. If the study were to be repeated, different priorities would undoubtedly emerge. Responses could also differ in countries with less stable governments, where, consequently, there is greater apprehension about the status of government finances. The response of the users and the conclusions of the above survey suggest the architecture of financial information in the current context.

Information Pyramid

Quintessentially, much of the information that users need comes from the basic budgetary accounts maintained within the government and associated economic data, as well as statistical data on the performance aspects of every organization. These data are homogeneous in that information for certain categories is provided for the government as a whole. But the needs of the users are heterogeneous in that they represent a variety of interests. For example, a member of the legislature may be interested, given the pork-barrel considerations associated with the appropriation of funds, in the amounts spent in his or her constituency. This may be of little interest to domestic investors. Despite this divergence, a core of information is needed for informed decision making about government finances. This core information is basically derived from government accounts and then rearranged or supplemented by other data.

For purposes of analysis, it is useful to reiterate the distinction between government users and all others. Within the government, the central and spending agencies and the audit (which is frequently an independent institution) are distinguished. Outside the executive branch of government, the legislature is viewed as one group—a separate entity with its own legal and judicial powers—and other groups are the securities dealers (or investors), the media, special interest groups, and the public. These groups do not have formal legal powers, but their views have a substantial impact on the functions of a government. Finally, because governments now operate

---

[4]In a report entitled *Objectives of Financial Reporting*, published a year after the above survey, the Governmental Accounting Standards Advisory Board (1987) identified the three primary users: the public, legislative and oversight bodies, and investors and creditors. In this process, the Accounting Standards Board has excluded the needs of the users within the government (United States, Federal Accounting Standards Advisory Board, 1993c).

Table 12. Users' Needs

Category	Legislative Users	Public and Media	Government Planners and Managers	Economists	Corporate Users	Lenders and Securities Dealers
Need for annual report	X	X	X	X	X (in summary form)	X (overall summary stressed)
Recognition of physical assets	X	X	X	X	Divided views	Divided views
Comprehensive government-wide accounts (including enterprises)	X	X	X	X	X	X
Actuarial liabilities for employee pensions	—	X	X	X	—	X
Actuarial liability of ongoing social programs	X	X	X	X	X	X
Reporting gold holdings of government	—	—	—	X	X	X
Accrual of tax revenues	—	X	Ambivalent	—	—	X
Tax expenditures	X	X	X	X	X	X
Budgetary outcome comparison of actual to estimates	X	X	X	X	X	X
Timeliness of report	X	X	X	X	X	X
Adjustment for inflation	Consistency stressed	X	Caution indicated	Yes	Not in favor because of past unsatisfactory experience	Not in favor

Measures of deficit	Clarity and consistency essential	Should be shown in terms of different measures	Several measures prefered	Several measures preferred	Several measures preferred	Several measures preferred
Asset valuation	Market and economic value stressed	—	—	—	—	X
Performance information	X	X	X (but not as part of annual financial statement)	X	—	X (but with reservation)
Disaggregated information	By program and region	Importance of detail stressed	X	X	X	Aggregated information preferred
Cash and accrual information	Both needed	Both needed	Cash	Both needed	Cash	Cash

Source: United States, General Accounting Office, and Canada, Office of the Auditor General (1986).
Note: X indicates the needs of the user group.

in an economically integrated world, aid donors have an important role in the fiscal life of some countries and therefore need to be recognized as a separate category. Similarly, given the network of relations with international organizations, governments are also obliged to furnish a good deal of financial information on their activities.

User groups are illustrated in Diagram 4, and their requirements are shown in Table 13. In terms of their role in, and impact on, decision making, these users may be regrouped into two categories—those that are involved in day-to-day decision making about the macroeconomic management of the country, and those whose views and actions could significantly influence, usually with a lag, a country's finances. The former group comprises the government, the legislature, and the donors, and the latter includes the media, special interest groups, and the public. The requirements of the former are directly related to their role as decision makers and they thus need information on a more regular basis. The latter group is more varied, and each subgroup is likely to have a specific concern rather than an interest in the full picture. The choice of analytical framework to meet their needs is therefore a key issue.

Analytical Framework of Financial Reporting

The first step in delineating the analytical framework of financial reporting is to determine the basic level of information to be collected and then aggregated so as to assess a government's overall operations. The basic, or reporting, entity can be based on several perspectives. From the point of view of macroeconomic management, the framework would include all units that are funded by public moneys and whose transactions result in the provision of goods and services or otherwise have an impact on the economy. Inherent in this approach are three levels of government: central government, comprising ministries, departments, agencies, and bureaus, which function as instruments of policy management; general government, comprising the central government and the regional and local governments, each of which has financial sovereignty and related autonomy; and the public sector, comprising general government and public enterprises that are either owned or controlled by governments at different levels. Economic analysts both inside and outside the government prefer to have aggregate data in terms of these levels.

The accounting point of view brings a different dimension to the discussion. The Governmental Accounting Standards Advisory Board (United States, 1993c, pp. 107 and 108) suggests that the entity should be

Diagram 4. Architecture of Government Financial Information

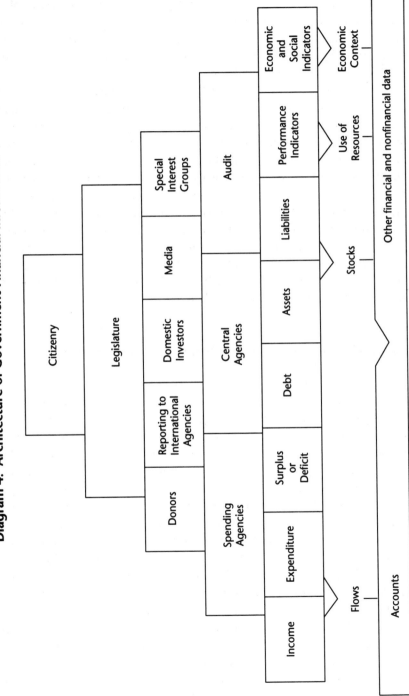

Table 13. Financial Information Users and Their Broad Needs

Category of Users	Purpose	Features
Outside the executive branch of government		
Legislative users	• To ascertain how the approved budget is being implemented; • To have appropriate information on the basis of which further legislation may be considered; • To be kept informed about possible major developments in the economy; and • To provide information about specific benefits flowing into each member's constituency from government operations.	Need periodic reports about trends in revenues, expenditures, and pattern of financing. A set of key financial indicators is to be presented periodically. This periodic information may need to be supplemented by other data that may be relevant for the approval of new policies and related financial appropriations. Full accounts must also be submitted, in some cases to a public accounts committee, for approval. In other cases, data must be submitted to departmental or appropriation committees to facilitate their review.
Citizens	• To form an opinion about the performance of the government as a guide at the time of elections. • To use the information on government performance for making decisions about personal finances.	Need periodic reports about the financial status of the government. Also prefer to be informed about any impending major developments in the economy.
Media	TV and print media report the announcements of the government and its activities. They need information on financial indicators and to assess the performance of the government and the economy. Since the media frequently carry out their own independent investigations, the data published by the government should be comprehensive and reliable.	Media tend to place more importance on reader/viewer-friendly approach and thus tend to use fewer technical terms and more graphics. The media need disaggregated data so that the choices before the government and the public can be made clear. Topical issues tend to get more coverage, frequently at the expense of more substantive matters.
Policy analysts	This group represents universities, independent institutions, and other think tanks. While they have several common objectives with the media, this group seeks to provide more substantive and objective analyses. They may seek not merely an analysis of the choices but also the impact, including the costs of environmental effects.	Their needs relate to more disaggregated data and longer time series and may cover areas that are not generally covered in the annual accounts. They may need data on taxes by groups of payees defined in terms of economic characteristics, and on the details of some programs. Their needs cannot always be anticipated and thus may require more diverse efforts.

Special interest groups	The purposes are wide ranging and each group may have its own objectives. Thus, taxpayers, customers, clientele groups of public services, employees of the government, suppliers and contractors that supply goods and services to the government and provide publicly funded services, and international voluntary organizations have different interests.	The interests of each group are different, and the only common denominator is the government budget or accounts or other periodic data. Given the diversity in the users, no single document is likely to prove adequate. All the same, the documents reflect the established need for a substantial pool of financial information.
Other levels of government	In countries with regions, states, provinces, municipalities, and other layers of subnational governments, users seek an understanding of the impact of the central or federal operations on their activities in general, and particularly on their ability to raise more resources through borrowing.	The need is for regular disaggregated information about the budget and its implementation.
Economists	Some of the needs of economists are covered in the above categories. In general, they are engaged in short- and medium-term analysis and forecasting, long-term analysis and forecasting, and special studies.	Users need data on an accrual and a cash basis for the central and general governments. More reliance is placed on the government tables included in the national income accounts. They prefer to have government revenues by type, expenditures by type and function, assets and liabilities including data on tax expenditures, and contingent liabilities.
Corporate users	This category includes all industrial, manufacturing, and commercial activities (excluding financial institutions considered below). Users' main interest is to plan their own production activities (as many are engaged in the sale of services to the public—see also special interest groups above) and to explore the feasibility of additional investment, tax planning, and related activities.	They seek detailed information on government outlays, status of projects, and future plans for spending and raising resources.
Lenders and securities dealers	This category represents both domestic and international groups that invest moneys in government bills and securities.	Their primary needs are (1) a forecast of macroeconomic balances (and in the event of persistent imbalances, the efforts that are proposed to rectify the situation), and (2) government's cash requirements during the year and related phasing of their borrowing requirements.

Table 13 *(concluded)*

Category of Users	Purpose	Features
Foreign donors	In several countries, foreign aid is a key component of budget financing.	They need more data on the general debt-servicing capacity of the recipient as well as detailed documentation of the projects and programs proposed for financing. In addition to data on budgetary operations, information is also needed on a wide variety of other economic aspects of the government.
International organizations and financial institutions	Their objective is to publish comparable and consistent data on government operations.	Methodology is frequently specified by the collecting agency. In most cases, the provision of data would involve a rearrangement of the building blocks to conform with the methodology specified.
Within the executive branch of government		
Central agencies	These include the ministries of finance and planning and, in some cases, the central bank. Their primary purpose is to monitor developments in the economy and, more specifically, trends in revenues, expenditures, and debt.	The corrective action that can be taken by the central agencies crucially depends on the regular flow of financial information. Data must be comprehensive, disaggregated, and timely. But not all details produced by the spending agencies are relevant for the needs of the central agencies.
Revenue managers	These include the tax-collecting agencies of the government. Information is needed about the operations of each functional area and at each organizational level so as to facilitate supervision.	Data must include information on amounts collected, lags in collection, delinquency in the filing of returns, and the areas where delinquency has arisen.
Foreign aid management	In countries where foreign aid is dominant, special agencies are set up to ensure coordination between donors and project authorities. The coordinating divisions are charged with the responsibility of fully utilizing the estimated aid while complying fully with the donor-specified conditionality.	Data are needed on major foreign aid flows, as well as on the status of contracts, submission of documentation for claiming reimbursement from donors, and on analysis of the linkages between the budget and foreign aid.
Debt and liability management	The role of short- and long-term liabilities has become more varied, complex, and important. Data are needed on the borrowing programs of the government and on developments in the domestic and external credit markets.	Management of government cash flows has become an important task. The ability of the government to make a dent in the escalating costs of borrowing depends on the flow of information.

Budget forecasting and rolling budgets	A major part of government outlays reflects commitments and policy decisions already made and laws on the statute book. Regular data are needed to update these estimates and to organize them on a rolling basis.	Data are needed for each functional and program expenditure in terms of economic type or other relevant profile (running costs of program or operation and maintenance expenditures of completed projects and programs).
Spending agencies	The needs of these agencies are more specific. They are responsible in many cases for compiling primary accounts. The objective is to monitor budget implementation to identify leads and lags, make cash forecasts, process additional budget forecasts when necessary, and ensure prudent management.	The collective role of the spending agencies is a crucial one in overall government financial management. Each agency requires an internal management information system that facilitates an ongoing, organized review of policy and financial aspects of all operations.
Project reporting	The implementation of major projects may have a significant effect on the overall budgetary outcome. The objective therefore is to monitor these projects at various levels—spending agencies, central agencies, and foreign aid agencies.	Projects have a threefold task: (1) schedule reporting on progress made in the acquisition of materials and land and in construction; (2) cost reporting on cost overruns and the methods envisaged for financing them; and (3) compliance reporting on the fulfillment of donors' conditions specified as a part of project financing. Data needed transcend the traditional borders of accounting and include several administrative elements.
Performance reporting	Agencies are required in many countries to produce (and publish) performance data in addition to their expenditure plans. The purpose is to analyze the efficiency of use of allotted resources.	These performance data differ from one agency to another. Most seek to examine and explain the input-output-outcome relationships and their accounting implications in terms of costs of operations.
National income accounts	Government accounts form the first step in the compilation of national income accounts for the central and general governments.	As noted in earlier chapters, accounts produced within the government may need several adjustments and supplementary efforts (to gather additional detail) to be suitable for inclusion in the national income accounts.
Audit	Accounts in most governments are required to be audited by independent audit institutions both during the year and at the end of the year.	Covers a wide ground, and detailed data may be needed at each step of the process.

defined with reference to the accountability perspective, arguing that "financial reporting based on accountability should enable the financial statement reader to focus on the body of organizations that are related by a common thread of accountability to the constituent citizenry." According to the Accounting Standards Board, these organizations are those whose elected officials are accountable for their actions and that are legally separate and fiscally independent. But the application of these criteria is complicated by the inherent ambiguity of determining legally separate identification and fiscal independence. At a practical level, the entity is one that is a primary government (the term "primary" could have many meanings and may include a school district, a local government, or a central government) and its organizations for which the primary government is financially accountable.

A strict application of this rule could, however, mean that some extrabudgetary funds may not be consolidated with the operations conducted through the budget because each fund has its own law and, in some cases, financial independence. In anticipation of these issues, the Accounting Standards Board (1993c, p. 109) added that the primary government should also include "other organizations for which the nature and significance of their relationship with the primary government are such that exclusions would cause the reporting entity's financial statements to be misleading or incomplete." This provision provides flexibility and is equal, in its intent, to the perspective of macroeconomic managers, which comprise all agencies that are effectively used as instruments of government policy.

Two other perspectives need to be considered: the organizational perspective, or that of the spending agencies; and the perspective of budgetary accounting—that is, of the central agencies in the government. Spending agencies focus primarily on their own activities, programs, and projects. Their view is conditioned by the organizational responsibility to procure and manage resources in their policy sphere. It is for this reason that the head of an agency in the British-type administrative system is designated the chief accounting officer as well as its civilian head with integrated responsibilities for policies and finances. Such agencies naturally concentrate on areas of vital importance for their financial management. Although one of the reasons that the spending agencies furnish financial information is "to assist in making comparisons among alternative ways of providing similar services,"[5] in practice, this function becomes the responsibility of the central agencies.

---

[5]United States, Federal Accounting Standards Advisory Board (1994b), p. 3.

The central agencies need financial information, first, to be fully congruent with the budget, and second, at a disaggregated level, to be anchored in responsibility or cost centers and in projects and programs. Budgetary accounts are distinct from treasury accounts. The former are rooted in the budget categories, while the latter are the accounts of the budgetary transactions and can include deposit accounts.

These different perspectives are rooted in the organizational responsibility of the agency seeking information. Inevitably, there may be some overlap and lack of consistency. This would imply that the same accounting information may have to be expanded beyond the core elements to meet the special requirements of the agencies. In operational terms, disaggregated information must then be aggregated or rearranged to conform with the needs of each user group. Experience in a number of countries shows that, because of the legal ambiguity about the entity or primary level of government, certain important elements of government activities may be overlooked. One such major exception is the reporting on extrabudgetary funds. In the economies in transition, as well as in many developing countries, financial reports often exclude the transactions of these funds. But this exclusion could well mean that frequently more than one-fourth of public outlays remain unreported. Similarly, the exclusion of the treasury account as, for example, in Italy, of the investment funds maintained by oil producing countries in the Middle Eastern region, or of Fiscal Government Loan Program operations in Japan, could well create a misleading picture of overall finances. As a result, concepts like budgetary surplus or deficit computed with reference to narrow bases tend to be robbed of their intrinsic utility. For this purpose, these funds should be added on, and it should be explicitly stated that they are being covered.

Yet another aspect of the accounting framework relates to the operations of public enterprises. It is contended, particularly by special interest groups and the media, that in economies with large public enterprises the distinction between government and enterprises is often arbitrary. In some countries, enterprises are used to pursue noncommercial objectives and to provide social services that would otherwise not receive government funding. If limits are set on the government budget deficit as part of stabilization-oriented fiscal policies, enterprises may continue to be used to provide services. Moreover, the balances of the government budget are often adversely affected by enterprise finances. This strong relationship between government and enterprises should therefore be recognized and information provided on the consolidated picture of enterprises.

A consolidation of finances and related reporting of the government and enterprises could, however, obscure the reality of both. The surpluses of enterprises could compensate for shortfalls in government budgets and vice versa. It is therefore appropriate that separate data for each enterprise be consolidated at a sectoral level for the profit and loss accounts and balance sheets as illustrated in Tables 14 and 15. This information would facilitate the appraisal of the financial health of each enterprise but would not divulge the more complex relationships between government and enterprises, particularly those relating to the tasks discreetly assumed by enterprises on behalf of governments.[6] These circumstances require a more organized response to the changing needs of user groups.

Purpose, Form, and Frequency

The content and form of financial reports are dependent, to a large extent, on the specific purposes of the user. In this context, users may be grouped into two broad categories: (1) legislative oversight bodies, and (2) agencies within the government. The former group may also be considered to represent the public, the media, and associated special interest lobbies. The latter group includes the central and spending agencies within the executive branch of the government. To meet the requirements of both groups, major changes have been made in the form and content of reports.

Legislative oversight bodies will differ depending on how a legislature functions. Some legislatures can only discuss the financial proposals of the government but cannot alter them in any way (for example, Egypt). In France, the legislature can make changes at the program level but cannot reduce revenues or increase expenditures beyond the aggregates proposed by the Government. Other types of legislature (such as those largely modeled on the British parliamentary tradition) have the right to appropriate moneys, but any major change that deviates from the proposals made by the executive is viewed as an expression of lack of confidence, obliging the government, in most cases, to resign. Some legislatures have the power to revise any element of the budget proposed by the executive branch. Although, in the final analysis, the budget in

---

[6]In most cases, enterprises are required by law to submit financial reports. But these are often disparate in quality and timeliness. Sometimes (for example, in Bangladesh, India, Pakistan, and Sri Lanka), consolidated reports are produced for the public enterprise sector. When consolidated reports are prepared, they permit an appraisal of the public sector as a whole.

Table 14. Public Enterprises: Operating, Profit, and Loss Account

	Year
Operating income	
Total financial resources	
Less charges varying with income	
Discounts	
Commissions	
Taxes	
Net operating income	
Less variable costs	
Materials	
Labor	
Other services	
Variable operating margin	
Materials	
Labor	
Other services	
Less short-run fixed costs	
Materials	
Labor	
Other services	
Short-run operating margin	
Less long-run fixed costs	
Depreciation of physical assets	
Amortization of intangible assets	
Other	
Operating margin before interest	
Less interest	
Operating margin after interest	
Add/less nonoperating items	
Subsidies	
Miscellaneous incomes	
Miscellaneous expenses	
Extraordinary incomes	
Extraordinary expenses	
Profit/loss before tax	
Less tax on profits	
Profit/loss after tax	

such cases is subject to approval by the country's chief executive, the legislature plays a dominant role.

Changes

The changes referred to earlier have mainly taken place in the legislative systems modeled on the British Parliament. The changes are in two

Table 15. Public Enterprises: Balance Sheet

Assets
  Noncurrent assets
  1. Physical assets
       Operating assets (net)
         Gross
         Less provision for depreciation
       Nonoperating assets
         Assets under construction
         Surplus and idle assets
  2. Monetary assets
       Equity investments
       Long-term loans
  3. Intangible assets

  Current assets
  1. Physical assets
       Inventories
         Finished goods
         Work in progress
         Raw materials
         Operating materials
         Maintenance stores
         Others
  2. Monetary assets
       Debtors
         Trade
         Others
       Short-term investments
       Bank balances
       Cash in hand

Liabilities
  Noncurrent liabilities
  1. Equity
       Contributed capital
       Reserves
         Revenue reserves
         Unappropriated balances of profit and loss account
         Capital reserves
           Asset revaluation reserves
           Others
  2. Long-term debt
       Gross
       Less current maturities (one year or less)
  3. Other noncurrent balances
       Deferred taxation provision
  Current liabilities
    Long-term debt dues
      Current maturities
      Arrears
    Short-term borrowings
    Interest payable
      Current
      Arrears
    Taxes (on profile)
    Dividends payable
    Bonuses payable
    Deposits payable
    Trade creditors

areas—the material submitted to "departmental select committees" and the content of the financial statements submitted at the end of the fiscal year.

One vexatious question long associated with parliamentary control has been the role of the legislature in the approval of the budget. It has been held that when the budget arrives at the legislature, it is in a completed form and that it is too late for the legislature to make a major contribution or play a constructive role. Consequently, the passage of the budget and associated financial legislation is considered a formality, more symbolic than substantive. In some countries (for example, India), the bulk of recent financial legislation has been enacted by voice vote in the "guillotine hour"—that is, before the scheduled closure of the parliamentary debate.

With a view to assigning a more constructive role to the legislature, "estimates committees" (special committees comprising members of the legislature) were created to review departments' current policies. Because this response did not deliver the hoped-for result, the committees were replaced, in the United Kingdom, by select committees on expenditure. These suffered the same fate as the estimates committees and have yielded place to departmental select committees. These committees (which have their counterparts in other similar parliamentary bodies) review selected aspects of the activities of each department, which are generally chosen with reference to three criteria—to seek explanations of unusual changes in expenditures, to review issues previously examined but unresolved, and to examine areas where changes in policy or other conditions require a reassessment of budgeted amounts.[7]

Departmental Report

With a view to meeting the needs of these committees, departments are obliged to submit, along with their budget, a "departmental report" outlining their goals and activities.[8] Although these departmental reports can be structured in various ways, their purpose is to provide detailed descriptions of aims, objectives, priorities, expenditure plans for future years, an enumeration of major policy develop-

---

[7]See Likierman (1988, p. 150 and following pages) for a detailed description of the tasks and procedures of these committees.

[8]These departmental reports had their origins in the United Kingdom in Public Expenditure White Papers.

Table 16. Performance Data: U.K. Hospital Activity Statistics

Category	1992–93	1993–94
Ordinary admissions		
General and acute		
Acute		
Geriatric		
Maternity		
All specialties		
Day cases		
General and acute		
All specialties		
New outpatients		
Acute		
Geriatric		
Maternity		
Mental illness		
Learning disabilities		
Ward attenders		
Occupied bed days		
Mental illness		
Learning disabilities		
Average length of episode (days)		
Acute		
Geriatric		

Source: United Kingdom, Department of Health and Office of Population Censuses and Surveys (1994c, p. 42).

ments in each area, and detailed data on performance and the use of resources.[9]

The reports are intended to provide a basis for informed discussion both by the committee and, when appropriations are taken up for voting, by the full legislature. These reports have been, and are being, refined every year in response to comments from the public. Inasmuch as they describe the efforts the agencies are making to ensure economical use of resources, the reports represent a window of opportunity for agencies to explain themselves to the public. In particular, the recent emphasis on providing consistent performance data (see Table 16) appears to have whetted, at least in part, the public's appetite for increased accountability. The reports provide an empirical foundation for informed appraisal, careful scrutiny, and comment. Their effectiveness in terms of changes in government policies and programs is more problematic, because it depends partly on the use made of the material by the committee and partly on

[9]In India, performance budgets of each ministry are submitted to the parliament as supplemental information.

the broad working relationship between the committee and the government. Although these committee reports are rarely "accepted" or "rejected" explicitly, there are cases in which the recommendations have been accepted "in principle." Moreover, what is not accepted may also contribute to departmental policy changes over time.

Annual Appropriation Accounts

The second major change refers to the submission of the government's financial statements. As noted earlier, in some systems, these annual accounts, which basically follow the structure of budgetary appropriations, must be reviewed and approved, along with audit reports, by public accounts committees. There has been a growing feeling over the years, however, that the appropriation accounts have not revealed the government's financial situation. As discussed in previous chapters, these accounts were mostly done on a cash basis and were not designed to reveal the government's asset and liability position, much less contingent liabilities that may need to be redeemed sooner rather than later. Overall, the accounts were not considered completely transparent and accurate. For these and associated reasons, the demand has grown for an annual financial report that goes beyond the appropriation accounts and provides a broad and complete picture of the government's varied and complex activities and resulting overall financial position. Such a report would also serve as the basis (and not a substitute) for the more detailed information the government now provides in a number of different financial documents. The annual report represents an attempt to provide comprehensiveness, cohesiveness, and, it is hoped, clarity.

The annual financial report generally includes several statements on a government's operations (Table 17), financial position (Table 18), cash flows (Table 19), borrowings (Table 20), commitments (Table 21), and contingent liabilities (Table 22). In New Zealand, for example, these statements are submitted to the legislature twice a year—for the first six months (these statements are not audited) and at the end of the fiscal year.

Users Within the Government

The users within the government are the central and spending agencies, which have a reciprocal relationship: their actions reinforce each other in their respective spheres of activity. The central agencies are

Table 17. New Zealand: Operating Statement

Revenue
  Levied through the Crown's sovereign power
    Direct taxation
    Indirect taxation
    Other
      Total
  Earned through the Crown's operations
    Investment income
    Sales of goods and services
    Other operational revenue
      Total

Total revenue

Expenses
  By functional classification
    Social services
    Education
    Administration
    Health
    Foreign relations
    Development of industry
    Transport
    Finance costs
    Net foreign exchange losses

Total expenses

Revenue less expenses
    Surplus attributable to state-owned enterprises and Crown entities
    Dividends and other distributions
    Net surplus attributable to state-owned enterprises and Crown entities
    Dividends and other distributions

  Net surplus attributable to state-owned enterprises and Crown entities

Operating balance

Source: New Zealand (1993).

primarily responsible for formulating and overseeing the implementation of macroeconomic policies. The spending agencies are responsible for implementing sectoral policies and managing the funds assigned to them. This traditional relationship has acquired a new dimension in the context of economic stabilization. Stabilization policies involve compliance with quantitative ceilings on expenditures, debt, and the budget deficit. Compliance has imposed additional tasks on the central agencies: pursuit of stabilization requires a regular monitoring system that covers the various aspects of the spending agencies' activities.

As users, the central agencies use four types of data: (1) budgetary data, (2) data on financial position, (3) data unique to the context or

Table 18. New Zealand: Statement of Financial Position

Assets
  Current assets
    Cash and bank balances
    Investments
    Receivables and advances
    Inventories
      Total

  Noncurrent assets
    Investments
    Receivables and advances
    State-owned enterprises and Crown entities
    Physical assets
    Intangible assets
      Total

Total assets

Liabilities
  Current liabilities
    Payables and provisions
    Pension liabilities
    Borrowings
      Total

Term liabilities
  Payables and provisions
  Currency issued
  Pension liabilities
  Borrowings
    Total term liabilities

Total liabilities

Total assets less total liabilities

Crown balance
  Accumulated operating balance
  Revaluation reserve

Crown balance

Source: New Zealand (1993).

environment of each agency, and (4) performance data. It has been noted in previous chapters that several checks and balances operate between the central and spending agencies in regard to the release of budgetary authority and associated funds. Reports are needed on how the released funds have actually been used, whether they have been within the specified ceilings, and, if not, the reasons. This type of data emanates directly from the journal and ledger entries of each agency, which are rearranged in an analytical way for use by the central agencies. The central agencies also receive information from the financial

Table 19. New Zealand: Statement of Cash Flows

Cash flows from operations
  Cash provided from
    Direct taxation
      Individuals
      Companies
      Withholding taxes
      Other direct taxation
        Total

    Indirect taxation
      Goods and services tax
      Excise duties
      Other indirect taxation
        Total

    Other receipts
      Interest, profits, and dividends
      Other operating receipts
        Total

Total cash provided

  Cash disbursed to
    Social services
    Education
    Health
    Administration
    Development of industry
    Foreign relations
    Transport
    Finance costs

Total cash disbursed

Net cash flows from operations

Cash flows from investing activities
  Cash provided from
    Sale or repayment of advances and investments
    Sale of physical assets

Total cash provided

  Cash disbursed to
    Purchase of investments and advances
    Purchase of physical assets

Total cash disbursed

Net cash flows from investing activities

Cash flows from financing activities
  Cash provided from
    Issue of circulating currency
    Issue of government stock
    Other borrowing in New Zealand dollars
    Foreign currency borrowing
    Other items

Total cash provided

Table 19 *(concluded)*

Cash disbursed to
  Repayment of government stock
  Repayment of other borrowing in New Zealand dollars
  Repayment of foreign currency borrowing
  Major project refinancing
  Other items

Total cash disbursed

Net cash flows from financing activities

Net movement in cash held

Opening cash balance
  Reserve Bank of New Zealand opening cash balance
  Foreign exchange losses on opening cash balance

Closing cash balance

Source: New Zealand (1993).

institutions about the overall status of government finances. These reports enable the central agencies to anticipate developments, including
cash needs, and to be prepared to deal with them. The information so
collected is not limited to the budget but may include reports on public
enterprise finances depending on their role in the economy. This traditional task has been facilitated during recent years by access to computerized systems of data maintenance.

The reports on budgetary compliance do not necessarily fully reveal
an agency's financial status. The principle of stewardship, which is a
guiding force for financial disclosure, requires that agencies also submit
statements aimed at indicating their financial position. This information
would show how the agencies' financial conditions have changed and
how further changes may be anticipated. This task is partly achieved
through the balance sheets and income and expenditure statement referred to earlier. However, these statements need additional details about
assets and liabilities.

In the United States, measures have been taken to make the necessary
information available. Each agency is required to prepare three statements: a statement of financial position (Table 23), a statement of operations and changes in net position (Table 24), and a statement of cash
flows (Table 25). These must be furnished at the end of each fiscal year.
The full impact of these statements on the agencies' ability to manage
their finances and on the capacity of the public and other outside users
has not yet been assessed. There is, however, a demand for future reports

Table 20. New Zealand: Statement of Borrowings

Outstanding debt
  New Zealand dollars
    Government stock
    Treasury bills
    Retail stock
    Reserve bank bills
    Loans and foreign exchange contracts
      Total
  Foreign currency debt
    U.S. dollars
    Japanese yen
    Deutsche mark
    Pounds sterling
    Swiss francs
    European currency units
    Other currencies
      Total

Total outstanding debt

Offsetting marketable securities and deposits
  New Zealand dollars
  U.S. dollars
  Japanese yen
  Deutsche mark
  SDRs (IMF)
  Pounds sterling
  Swiss francs
  Other

Total marketable securities and deposits

Source: New Zealand (1993).
Note: Information is also provided about the intra-year movements in the above categories. In addition, data are provided on the maturity profiles of debt.

to provide more than an indication of the financial position—that is, present a broader, more forward-looking document that examines "financial condition."[10] This expanded concept will involve additional information about the likely impact of such variables as environmental degradation, relative competitiveness, productivity of the economy, and expected changes in demographic patterns.

This concept has since been given a more concrete form in terms of a statement or statements on investment in other physical capital and intellectual capital,[11] including a statement on selected future claims on resources. Although laudable in its effort to provide a more comprehensive picture of government finances, the concept may be considered to

---

[10]See United States, Federal Accounting Standards Advisory Board (1993c), pp. 58–59.
[11]See United States, Federal Accounting Standards Advisory Board (1994b), pp. 13–15.

Table 21. New Zealand: Statement of Commitments

By type
  Capital commitments
    Specialist military equipment
    Land and buildings
    Other plant and equipment
    Investments
    State-owned enterprises and Crown entities
      Total
  Operating commitments
    Noncancelable accommodation leases
    Other noncancelable leases
    Noncancelable contracts for the supply of goods and services
    Other operating commitments
    State-owned enterprises and Crown entities
      Total
Total commitments

By functional classification
  Foreign relations
  Development of industry
  Administration
  Education
  Social services
  Transport
  Health
  State-owned enterprises and Crown entities
Total commitments

By term
  One year or less
  From one to two years
  From two to five years
  Over five years
Total commitments

Source: New Zealand (1993).

exceed the conventional realm of government accounting. The concerns of government central agencies, which are narrower and more specific, are likely to revolve around movements in cash and other monetary assets, balances with the treasury, investments, receivables, physical assets, payables, and the net position. Similarly, obligations incurred, unobligated balances, unpaid obligations, and excess of expenditures over revenues and other financing resources are likely to receive special attention.[12]

The financial position of an agency is routinely affected by changes in policy and related legislation, on the one hand, and, on the other hand, by

---

[12]Separate budgetary accounting and related reporting may not be required where the budget categories are structured (as in Chile) on the lines of a balance sheet.

Table 22. New Zealand: Statement of Contingent Liabilities

Quantifiable contingent liabilities
    Guarantees and indemnities
    Uncalled capital
    Legal proceedings and disputes
    Other contingent liabilities
Total

Source: New Zealand (1993).
Note: A list of nonquantifiable contingent liabilities is also provided. In addition, two other statements on unappropriated expenditure and expenses (expenditure in excess of or without appropriation by Parliament) and trust money are provided.

specific developments in the availability of items commonly consumed by agencies. For example, a scarcity of building materials affects the activities of the construction agency. These changes may have a greater impact on future budgets and thus need to be reported so that the central agencies have a widened perspective on the future needs of the agency.

Finally, as has been repeatedly noted, accountability now requires that performance be reported both to the central agencies and to the public to assist them in their respective evaluations. Performance data include costs, measures of accomplishment, outputs, and outcomes.

All the above types of data are generated by the spending agencies, whose interests are identical to those of the central agencies. But the spending agencies are responsible for implementing projects and thus require more detail at every level, for example, at every stage of a construction project. In this regard, spending agencies usually have schedule reporting—a system that specifies the different stages of construction in terms of physical landmarks. The reports specify the progress made, slippage in construction schedules, new dates for completion, and the impact of such changes on cost. In addition, the spending agencies are involved in reconciling physical and financial aspects. Their policy goals depend on the physical progress made and its impact on the allotted finances.

While the central agencies also have an interest in the physical results, their major concern is financial. It is for this reason that major spending agencies in some governments have endeavored to set up their own management information systems that will be congruent with the larger financial information systems and, at the same time, generate additional detail in conformity with the requirements of each spending agency. The existence of management information systems (which was key to the financial management initiative organized in the United Kingdom) goes a long way in buttressing the purposes of financial management and in

Table 23. United States: Statement of Financial Position

	Year	Year
Assets		
Financial resources		
Fund balances with Treasury		
Cash		
Foreign currency		
Other monetary assets		
Investments, nonfederal		
Accounts receivable, net nonfederal		
Inventories held for sale		
Loans receivable, net nonfederal		
Property held for sale		
Other, nonfederal		
Intragovernmental items, federal		
Accounts receivable, net		
Loans receivable, net		
Investments		
Other		
Total financial resources		
Nonfinancial resources		
Resources transferable to Treasury		
Advances and prepayments, nonfederal		
Inventories not held for sale		
Property, plant, and equipment, net		
Other		
Total nonfinancial resources		
Total assets		
Liabilities		
Funded liabilities		
Accounts payable, nonfederal		
Accrued interest payable		
Accrued payroll and benefits		
Accrued entitlement benefits		
Lease liabilities		
Liabilities for loan guarantees		
Deferred revenue, nonfederal		
Pensions and other actuarial liabilities		
Other funded liabilities, nonfederal		
Intragovernmental liabilities		
Accounts payable, federal		
Debt		
Deferred revenue		
Other funded liabilities, federal		
Total funded liabilities		
Unfunded liabilities		
Accrued leave		
Lease liabilities		
Debt		
Pensions and other actuarial liabilities		
Other unfunded liabilities		
Total unfunded liabilities		
Total liabilities		
Net position		
Fund balances		
Revolving fund balances		
Trust fund balances		
Appropriated fund balances		
Less future funding requirements		
Net position		
Total liabilities and net position		

Source: United States, Office of Management and Budget (1992).
Note: Unless otherwise indicated, the statements are as of September 30 of each year. These statements are to be furnished by each department or agency and are then consolidated.

Table 24. United States: Statement of Operations and Changes in Net Position

	Year	Year
Revenues and financing sources		
Appropriations expensed		
Revenues from sales of goods and services		
To the public		
Intragovernmental		
Interest and penalties, nonfederal		
Interest, federal		
Taxes		
Other revenues and financing sources		
Less: taxes and receipts transferred to the treasuries of other agencies		
Total revenues and financing sources		
Expenses		
Program or operating expenses		
Cost of goods sold		
To the public		
Intragovernmental		
Depreciation and amortization		
Bad debts and write-offs		
Interest		
Federal financing bank/treasury borrowing		
Federal securities		
Other		
Other expenses		
Total expenses		
Excess (shortage) of revenues and financing sources over total expenses before adjustments		
Plus (minus) adjustments		
Extraordinary items		
Prior period adjustments		
Excess (shortage) of revenues and financing sources over total expenses		
Plus: unfunded expenses		
Excess (shortage) of revenues and financing sources over funded expenses		
Net position, beginning balance		
Plus (minus) nonoperating changes		
Net position, ending balance		

Source: United States, Office of Management and Budget (1992).

inspiring greater confidence in the adequacy of management and control systems in government agencies.

Issues in Transforming Financial Information

The discussion so far testifies to the growing interest in financial information produced by governments. The number and variety of users have

Table 25. United States: Statement of Cash Flows (Direct Method)

	Year	Year
Cash provided (used) by operating activities		
Cash provided		
Tax collections		
Sales of goods and services		
Interest and penalties		
Benefit programs		
Insurance and guarantee programs		
Other operating cash provided		
Total cash provided		
Cash used		
Goods and services		
Personal services and benefits		
Travel and transportation		
Rent, communications, and utilities		
Printing and reproduction		
Other contractual services		
Supplies and materials		
Insurance claims and indemnities		
Grants, subsidies, and contributions		
Other operating cash used		
Total cash used		
Net cash provided (used) by operating activities		
Cash provided (used) by investing activities		
Sale of property, plant, and equipment		
Purchase of property, plant, and equipment		
Sale of securities		
Purchase of securities		
Collection of long-term loans receivable		
Creation of long-term loans receivable		
Other investing cash provided (used)		
Net cash provided (used) by investing activities		
Appropriations (current warrants)		
Add		
Restorations		
Transfers of cash from others		
Deduct		
Withdrawals		
Transfers of cash to others		
Net appropriations		
Borrowing from the public		
Repayments on loans to the public		
Borrowing from the treasury and the Federal Financing Bank		
Repayments on loans from the Treasury and the Federal Financing Bank		
Other borrowings and repayments		
Net cash provided (used) by financing activities		
Net cash provided (used) by operating, nonoperating, and financing activities		
Fund balances with Treasury, cash, and foreign currency, beginning		
Fund balances with Treasury, cash, and foreign currency, ending		

Source: United States, Office of Management and Budget (1992).

expanded, as have their interests, partly because of the increasing complexity of economic management in the modern world. Indeed, some users have asserted their "right" to be informed.[13] In the years to come, as this right becomes more prominent and consolidated, governments will be obliged to take into account the users' changing information requirements. Governments and their accounting machinery must recognize this task explicitly and not merely provide information but also make the information more comprehensive and timely. Concomitantly, accounting agencies must reflect on the situation and evaluate their own ability to respond to users' rights. The design of existing information systems is a key issue in this process.

Design Issues

The architecture of any system reflects the needs and the ethos of the age in which it is established. The information system is no exception. Inevitably, then, these systems, when viewed at a later date, might appear obsolete and dysfunctional. In addition, they may be characterized by design flaws.

First, applying commercial formats to government accounting is a recurring issue. Now, however, there is greater agreement that commercial formats, albeit with adjustments, can be applied to government organizations. The anchoring of a set of theories in one field imparts authority to a set elsewhere if it can be anchored in the same procedures. Thus, the application of these formats should increase over time and acquire additional strengths and legitimacy. Will these formats supplant the existing appropriation accounts used by the legislature, or the established classification of government functions and publication of government finance data, or the details of public debt data published by central banks? Each of these presentations has its purpose and clientele. Through the application of commercial formats, the same facts would be further reinforced for some users. For some, commercial accounting approaches could provide additional clarity and an improved basis for comparison with the private sector. In the process, the traditional chasm between the accounting approaches of the public and private sectors may be substantially reduced.

---

[13]In a report issued in 1973, the American Institute of Certified Public Accountants noted that it was "fundamental and pervasive" that "the basic objective of financial statements is to provide information useful for making economic decisions," implying some user rights. Cited in Likierman (1989), p. 15.

Preparing accounts according to commercial formats would require changes in the orientation as well as in the organization of data.[14] Numbers would need to be compiled on both a cash and an accrual basis, and agencies would be obliged to compile data on their liabilities. During the transition, efforts may be geared toward arranging the blocks of information in commercial formats; the more important task will be to internalize the implications of these formats for purposes of financial management within government agencies. Provision of information would then be a natural by-product of the process, rather than the result of an independent effort. Fortunately, much of the transformation has been simplified by technology. The design of the information system should therefore be seen as an integral part of the larger design of the coverage, basis, classification, and cost computation tasks of the overall accounting machinery in government.

Second, experience shows that, far too often, central agencies and donors request detailed information that is not always directly related to their needs. In a survey conducted by the World Bank, it was concluded that in many countries where monitoring systems are operating, their main utility is not to the project manager but to the central and planning and finance ministries.[15] The study added that the highly centralized nature of the systems means "that they are seen primarily as an instrument for 'central agencies' to control managers—not a management tool to improve poor performance." According to the study, the information system responded more to the needs of donor agencies than to the needs of management. While the needs of central agencies are clearly established, the needs must be tempered by a recognition that the agencies can have little positive motivation to provide information that is not related to their own immediate and substantive concerns. The same factor could contribute to extensive doctoring of the data, which would effectively render them useless. As a principle, therefore, central agencies should seek information that is useful to the provider, and then, as an extension, to

---

[14]It is not productive to engage in a discussion of which one is superior. The traditional flow statements have their strengths as balance sheets aimed at the determination of the net worth of governments. The assets and liabilities may not fully capture the transactions that imply future tax obligations or those that imply future expenditures. The inclusion of items in assets of the government does not necessarily mean that they are capable of generating revenues. While the balance sheet is an indicator of the financial performance of public authorities, it does not serve, nor does it claim to serve, as a basis for determining whether governments are achieving their goals. It is necessary to recognize that accounting of deficits is only one important aspect, while the other important issue is the interpretation of deficits. Balance sheets offer another vantage point for analyzing the financial results of public policies; the analysis provided by balance sheets, however, is by no means the conclusive one.

[15]Ahmed and Bamberger (1989), pp. 8–9.

themselves. This underlines the need for a continuing dialogue between providers and users about the purposes of data.

Third, it needs to be reiterated that providing information involves costs (economists tend to consider them capital costs).[16] Potential improvements in the design of information systems need to be weighed against their affordability. In some cases, partial recovery of costs may be possible (through the sale of information, as some central statistical organizations of governments have done in recent years). However, to a large extent, changes are likely to be a burden on the taxpayer, leading inevitably to a phasing of improvements, if not to their abandonment. Cost constraints must be explicitly taken into account in determining the future organization of information.[17] Fourth, the timing of the release of information and the extent of information released (owing to confidentiality) are conditioned by the government's perception of the anticipatory actions by the economic agents.

Operational Issues

One of the major criticisms leveled against the financial information provided by government is that it becomes available only after a long delay, thereby reducing its usefulness for policymakers as well as for the public. Some countries have resolved this problem by instituting "flash reporting systems," under which the aggregates or the control totals are reported quickly to the policymakers. Unfortunately, these efforts represent a "band-aid" approach. A viable alternative is to review the accounting framework, with a view to eliminating systemic problems, and to install electronic processing machinery to accelerate compilation. This approach is actually being implemented in a number of countries.

An associated criticism of governments is that they manipulate data in a self-serving way. This can be avoided only if the users examine available information and publicize their results whenever the quality of information is found to be wanting. However well the system may have been designed, operational lapses and abuses are likely to reduce the usefulness of the product—in this case, information. In such circumstances,

---

[16]Arrow, for example, observes that a "characteristic of information costs is that they are in part capital costs; more specifically, they typically represent an irreversible investment." See Arrow (1983), p. 170.

[17]Until recently, the specification of accounting standards has not taken into account the cost aspects. In its most recent report (Exposure Draft, 1994c, p. 3), the U.S. Federal Accounting Standards Advisory Board suggested that the entity should ensure that all the relevant financial information is provided, subject to the constraints of cost.

modern democracies provide opportunities for the public to express their views and to pursue follow-up action. It is to be explicitly recognized that disclosure provides accountability to some while making available information to all interested. Government's interface with other economic agents may limit the information released.

6

Investing in Development: Implementation

The need for investing in the development of accounting systems, operational techniques, and procedures, as well as the need for upgrading technology, has been considered in detail in the preceding chapters. While some of these needs may seem self-evident, it is appropriate to recapitulate some of the arguments so that the directions of development, the content of needed improvements, and the ways in which improvement may be pursued can be put in proper perspective.

Do governments need to be convinced of the need to invest in developing their accounting systems? Although the sporadic efforts of some countries suggest that governments are already convinced of the value of such an investment and have even articulated sound plans for the purpose, there are others in which little or no effort has been made. Indeed, in some countries there are hardly any efforts. While the expanding scope of technical assistance provided by donors and international agencies may suggest that substantial reform is on the way, in reality, the situation is more reminiscent of the opening lines of Dickens's *A Tale of Two Cities*. It is the best of times for those governments pursuing measures aimed at strengthening their systems. What they have achieved so far represents the cutting edge of the accounting discipline. For other countries, it is the worst of times because efforts to strengthen accounting, having yielded few results, are faltering. For them, the question is: How can the effort be sustained if it proves to be costly and has not delivered the expected results?

The view taken thus far has been that governments must be convinced of the need for development in this area and then must dedicate themselves to renewed effort. The urgency arises for the following five reasons.

Fiscal welfare-oriented state. First, governments have in general moved from the fiscal-military state[1] to the fiscal welfare-oriented state. The former, which dominated the scene in the seventeenth and eighteenth

---

[1]The term is drawn from Brewer (1989), p. 18.

centuries in England, transformed government: it became the single largest player in the economy. This astonishing transformation also contributed to a steady expansion in the number of transcribers, copyists, and record keepers. Extended wars induced governments to raise funds through taxation and, more significantly, through borrowing from the public. If wars created a new class of investors and contractors, the financing of wars led to the emergence of a new class of financial interest holders, with growing investments in government bonds and securities. These interest holders, in turn, created a demand for more detailed and precise information about the operations of governments.

An inevitable by-product of these events was the inexorable growth in financial records and documents, and, in due course, the growth of accountancy in governments. Although the clerks responsible for accounting were looked down upon by the landed class, their stature steadily rose. The change in the composition of expenditures over the centuries and, more recently, the growth of funds for entitlements and welfare benefits have forged a new relationship between the state and its clients, transforming the state into one based on fiscal welfare. These new relationships have serious implications for financial accountability and, thus, for accounting.

Fiscal credibility. Owing to the movement in budget financing toward more reliance on domestic and external borrowing, governments have been obliged to establish credibility in their macroeconomic policies, particularly fiscal policies. In most countries, fiscal policy is at the heart of economic adjustment and can be successful only when it is perceived to be credible. When credibility is lacking, government operations become more costly. Credibility in turn should be rooted in the budgets and the periodic accounts published. The response of the investing public depends on the reliability of the fiscal information furnished by governments, and, in that context, accounts must be based on well-recognized standards. It is the scrupulous adherence to these standards that lends credibility to government fiscal operations. In turn, these standards have many implications for government accounts.

Fiscal rectitude. No amount of fiscal credibility would by itself lead to sustained economic adjustment. Governments must address existing problems. For example, they can address growing expenditures through policy measures and supporting efforts aimed at containing costs. The latter response is firmly rooted in the discipline of government accounting. An important consideration is the extent to which government accounting has addressed cost measurement and containment. In this area, what has been accomplished pales into insignificance relative to what remains to be done. Recent conceptual and practical advances in measuring costs in the private sector offer hope for their relevance for public organizations. Similarly, governments must maintain records that will alert them to the future magnitude of short- and long-term liabilities and their implications for fiscal policies. This internal fiscal rectitude can be generated only from improved accounting. Efforts to establish currency boards (which are, by definition, exempted from extending credit to governments) or to grant central banks more autonomy so that they are not obliged to accept the soft credit constraints sought by governments may have a beneficial impact on governments' approaches to accounting. More enduring results are likely to emerge when fiscal credibility is viewed as a problem to be addressed from within, through honest budgeting and sagacious accounting.

Changing tasks and patterns of control. The tasks of government, as noted, have changed, as have the patterns of expenditure management within public agencies. The issue then is to what extent accounting is able to reinforce patterns in expenditure management. Are, for example, the traditional financial statements furnished by the accounting agencies adequate to meet the needs of government expenditure managers? Are accounting methods sufficient to facilitate the evaluation of completed government programs and projects? Are accounting data useful in enabling the government and public policymakers to make decisions as to which services should be provided by in-house facilities and which should be contracted out? Is the accounting system generating adequate data about hidden liabilities that are likely to contribute to a serious and unexpected fiscal crisis for the state? Is the system generating data on the physical assets of the government and the need for maintaining these assets? Is the system addressing the issues of intergenerational equity? These issues have become an integral part of the methods of control of expenditure managers. These and other issues that have not yet emerged imply that the accounting profession and governments must look beyond the traditional appropriation accounts and statements on variations between budgeted and actual expenditure. If they do not seize this opportunity to respond to the challenges, accounting is likely to be viewed as having only historical value and as being obsolete in its approach and operations.

Organizational sclerosis. Another relevant question is whether the government accounting systems will be able to deliver services in the areas designated for them. Although the picture is changing somewhat, the perception of those inside and outside the government is that the accounts are published too late and with gaps and caveats that substantially reduce their usefulness. Slippages can occur for many reasons but when they become routine occurrences, then it is time to address them in the same way that a physician addresses a sick patient. Is the accounting system attempting to handle the tasks of the late twentieth century with tools that are at least a century old? Will investing in technology compensate for human failings and the systems' limitations? What complementary efforts and plans are needed to prepare the accounting systems for the application of available technology? Assuming that technology is available, is it being put to optimum use in government? If not, how can that increased utilization be achieved? Experience in many industrial and developing countries, as well as in economies in transition, shows that efforts to take advantage of technology are feeble and frequently lack overarching themes and relevant strategies.

These issues, which are gathering strength from one day to the next, need to be addressed before they gain hurricane force. Investment in development consists in preventing potential problems by addressing them through concerted improvements. Such investment recognizes explicitly three features. First, accounting has been evolving over the years, but those areas that have been neglected or were not given the necessary support must now be developed in a short time. It is an exercise in catching up rather than in running ahead of events in anticipation of the future. Second, accounting in government can no longer be pursued as an independent discipline with only peripheral contact with other disciplines that together contribute to public sector management. Rather, it should be recognized as an important component of the overall design of public expenditure management that interacts with other elements of the design. Third, this development is not a short-term phenomenon, but a long journey. Like other long journeys, it requires a good deal of preparation, experimentation, reappraisal, flexibility, and sustained effort throughout. It is a long-term process to build a bridge that will permit current and future generations to take full advantage of accounting in their daily life.

Design of Development

The design of development and the specific measures that governments should consider, which have been examined at length in the first five chapters of this book, may be recapitulated. Notwithstanding the inherent risks in the grouping of countries, it is advantageous to consider the design of development in terms of industrial countries, former centrally planned economies, and developing countries. The immediate tasks in industrial countries are to refine the recent applications (for example, balance sheets) and to seek their extended application to other levels of government. Along with this effort, the internal financial management capability in the spending agencies needs to be strengthened so that the implications of commercial formats are internalized by them in the management of their day-to-day activities.

Simultaneous efforts are indicated for the introduction of cost management systems. In the economies in transition from central planning, continued attention to the improvement of the payments system and to the assignment of management responsibilities to the spending agencies is indicated. For too long, the agencies functioned as mere operational arms of the planning ministry, with little need to analyze or evaluate their actions except to seek higher budget allocations for their activities and for the enterprises under their control. There cannot, however, be any progress in financial management unless and until the deservedly important role of the spending agencies is recognized and enhanced. Here, too, emphasis is needed on developing cost management systems for, without them, there is little prospect for major improvement in their public finances.

Accounting standards, which have tended in the past to distort tariff and tax policies, need a major overhaul. The developing countries, in particular, need to strengthen the technical infrastructure (use of computers) of financial management. Although some developing countries have made spectacular progress in the installation and effective use of computer technology in a short period, others are way behind in updating technology. The overall picture is therefore mixed. These countries have several tasks to address and governments must work together to develop accounting policies.

The specific components of improved accounting and their potential impact are illustrated in Table 26. The table also describes the possible impact of these measures on accountability (which inevitably depends in part on a country's political system and legislative tradition), on internal controls, on the cost of controls, and on overall fiscal management. The measures illustrated in the table can be divided into two categories—those that lend themselves to quick implementation and those that would involve more time and sustained effort. The former category includes improvements in payments systems, a substantially revised framework of relationships with the banking system, and improved financial information systems. Each case entails reviewing the existing systems, identifying the problem areas in light of the considerations discussed in the preceding chapters, and undertaking improvements. Cost-effectiveness should continue to be a consideration. Each of these areas would then have an objective or objectives formulated in terms of users' goals. It should be noted that some information needs, such as the preparation of balance

Table 26. Likely Impact of Effective Accounting Systems

Category	Greater Accountability	Internal Controls	Reduced Cost of Control	Impact on Overall Fiscal Management
Payment mode transformation	No direct impact	Contributes to effective cash management	Costs will be less over time	Beneficial
Improved relations with banking system	No direct impact	Induces more effective controls	Short-run costs may be high as all transactions will be transparent	Beneficial
Application of commercial type of accounting, including accrual	Improves understanding of assets and liability position and improves budgetary presentation	Increases spending agencies' financial consciousness	Conversion costs likely to be significant in the short term	Beneficial
Improved linkages with national income accounts	No direct impact	No direct impact	No impact; slight possibility of cost reduction	Improved understanding should contribute to strengthened analysis of policy options and impact
Improved foreign aid accounting	Improves accountability	Enhances control capacities	No direct impact	Contributes to substantial improvements
Cost measurement	Changes nature of accountability	Provides an empirical base for operation of controls	Could contribute to reduced costs of control over the medium term	Provides many anchors for resource allocation and utilization
Liability management	Improves accountability	Contributes to more meaningful controls	No direct impact	Contributes to a smoother policy environment
Accounting standards	Very helpful	Provides an improved framework	No direct impact	Helpful
Improved financial information systems	Very helpful	Very helpful	No direct impact	Very helpful

sheets, are contingent on the progress made in adapting commercial accounting practices to the government. These measures do not always involve an additional substantial investment in hardware. Rather, they imply pursuing specific goals more purposefully and utilizing the existing machinery to serve those goals.

Other measures, such as those linked to the adaptation of commercial accounting (which in most cases should also contribute to enhanced links with national income accounts), specification of methods of cost measurement, liability management, and accounting standards, are likely to take time because of the necessary administrative preparation. They may also require additional financing for the acquisition of computers and, in some cases, the approval of the legislature. Formulation of implementation plans over the longer term should, as far as possible, keep in view some of the inevitable tensions (stemming from the conflicting positions inherent in any bureaucracy).

First, the design of the investment program should be customized for the specific needs of the government and the level of its administrative development. Experience shows that governments tend to believe that they can do as well as other governments and therefore tend to emulate what others have done. Experience also shows that this approach can be a recipe for more problems at a later stage. From an institutional point of view, there is considerable commonality in the administrative systems of governments. Most have a legislature—although the role it plays can vary—a budget office, an agency responsible for payments, an agency entrusted with accounting tasks, and a central bank, functioning in most cases as the fiscal agent of the government. Most also have differing capacities of electronic data-processing technology. But within this broad framework, each government has a unique administrative culture and operating style. In fact, it can even be said that each government, like each individual, has a personality, which needs to be taken into account when implementation design is formulated.

Second, the primary focus of the legislature, the central agencies, and the spending agencies is likely to be on budgetary reporting—partly because it is a legal requirement in most cases and partly because it plays a central role in funding activities of the agencies. To the extent that the basis of the budget is different from that of the balance sheet approaches of commercial accounting, governments would need to have a double-track or multiple-track accounting system.

Third, the introduction of the core financial system, such as the general ledger system, is bound to be time consuming. Efforts aimed at standardization should be tempered by a recognition of the specific needs of the agencies. Although agencies have some common features in their operational systems, each has its own internal structure. To ensure that the proposed system reflects the needs of all agencies, they should participate in the design of the system from the outset. Agencies should be prepared for the introduction of the new system and any strategy developed should be a common one.

Fourth, the central agencies may try to take advantage of the opportunity to revamp the system to gain more power, consolidate their own hegemony, and secure more operational levers for their direct use. This tendency needs to be resisted. The new technology is intended to facilitate the tasks of the central agencies but not to oversee continuously the operations of the spending agencies. The accounting reforms are intended to buttress the role of the spending agencies and to secure more responsible financial behavior from them. It is important to restrain the inherent tendency to centralize and, instead, to promote decentralized operational management.

Finally, the formulation of accounting standards and the delineation of operational relationships between central and spending agencies may lead to overspecification, overprescription, and overregulation. The experience of many industrial countries shows that the autonomous accounting boards may be ambitious about the scope of the improvements to be made and this can be manifested in excessive prescription and regulation. Inevitably, such an exercise would be tantamount to sowing seeds for future discord and counterproductive efforts.

Implementation Lessons and Dilemmas

Efforts devoted to improvements in accounting are not new. Over the years, particularly since the 1960s, there have been, as noted earlier, sporadic attempts, which have provided some lessons. A short list of these lessons prepared in light of the assessments made by national authorities, professional groups, and international organizations is given below.

- Active and continuing support of a country's political authorities, namely, finance ministers, is essential for the success of the efforts.

- An integrated framework combining planning, budgeting, accounting, and reporting is essential so as to have a feasible program of improvement. This integrated strategy needs to be developed prior to implementation. Such a strategy should address the needs of internal and external resources and the technological underpinning of the proposed reforms.

- There is a need for a basic legal framework that establishes the tasks and defines the roles of each government agency.
- An effective project management structure should be in place.
- Too much reliance on one system can lead to neglect and, in some cases, deterioration of other systems.
- If the benefits of the proposed reform can be demonstrated early, additional commitment and support in a material form would become available. If, on the other hand, early identifiable benefits are unlikely to accrue, then the supporting nature of the reform and the systems need to be recognized.

These lessons, some of which may appear unexceptional, also raise fundamental dilemmas that must be addressed. The first dilemma faced in introducing any public sector reform is how to delineate the respective roles of the professional civil service and the political level of administration.

Political Support

Although in many countries the lack of political support is often claimed as the main cause of lackluster reform experience, it is also recognized that accounting as a discipline is considered too remote to attract the attention of politicians. In fact, many finance ministers maintain that they do not feel comfortable in supporting or defending draft legislation in the legislature because some of the proposed reforms are so loaded with technical jargon. The primary interest of the ministers is to be apprised of the benefits that the suggested reform would bring to the operations of the government and to the public. In the absence of any effort to establish these benefits, reform efforts are viewed cynically, either as an exercise in bureaucratic politics or as an attempt to comply with the suggestions of donors.

The availability of political support is contingent on the merits of the reform, and it is therefore useful to examine the substance of different types of reform.

Integrated or Specific Reform

A second, closely related dilemma is whether the reform should take an integrated approach or should be specific. Proponents of the integrated approach suggest that all the elements of government financial management are so closely interlinked that they cannot be addressed in isolation of each other. For example, improvements in accounting classification cannot be envisaged except in relation to the budget and the laws relating to its approval in the legislature. These linkages are recognized and some measures must be taken in tandem. Certain risks are also associated with an integrated approach, including that it could create unrealistic expectations. If benefits accrue late, the integrated approach could be labeled as overambitious and sinking under its own weight. The recent experience of many industrial countries (excluding Australia and New Zealand) suggests that each area of accounting needs to be examined separately and improvements made with due regard to the implications in other areas. To date, application of computer technology, efforts at introducing a variation of activity costing, improvements in the building blocks of financial information, and the introduction of balance sheets for government agencies have been undertaken somewhat independently. The choice should therefore not be posed as an ideological issue but as a pragmatic one that has to be answered with reference to the specific situation of a country.

Public Sector Reform or Financial Management Reform

A similar dilemma arises in answering the question: Should financial reform (integrated or specific) be undertaken as an integral part of the overall reform of the public sector or as a separate effort? Those who support the former approach suggest that the fiscal crisis in many countries induced their governments to undertake fiscal consolidation. This involves civil service reform (including retrenchment), improved accountability and financial management, reform of the state enterprise sector (including privatization), financial sector reform, reduction in military expenditures, and improved governance. The underlying goal is to improve the manner in which "power is exercised in the management of a country's economic and social resources for development."[2] The experiences of Australia, New Zealand, and several African countries are cited in support of this approach. Equally, it could be argued that financial management reform is justified even when no massive fiscal crisis is threatening the stability of a country. As the discussion in previous chapters shows, accounting in government has developed more slowly than other areas, and there is much to be done before it can be considered adequate and

---

[2]For a discussion of some of these questions, see World Bank (1994c).

responsive to the current and future tasks of a state. In practice, the reform choice depends on what is urgent and on what is feasible. But where there is a massive effort at reorienting the management of a country, there may be advantages in undertaking financial management improvement in tandem with public sector reform.

Imperatives of Technology or High-Tech Dependency

Some of the advances in accounting are substantially facilitated by the application of available computer technology, but governments' approaches toward this process reveal some ambivalence. On the one hand, it is recognized that technology is an imperative of the times and that not seizing the opportunity to modernize could result in irretrievable losses that cannot be compensated for in any way. Not having the requisite technology could erode the decision-making capability of governments and, as a consequence, the competitiveness of a country. Furthermore, the information requirements of a government in the modern world are such that it is no longer an issue of whether technology should be applied but one of what functions to apply it to and what hardware and software to procure. On the other hand, experience shows that there have been many glitches in the application of technology and that there has been a dependency on technology. Some even contend that the new technology may demand abilities that may not be locally available. These apprehensions need to be tempered by a recognition of the rapid progress made by some countries in internalizing the benefits of technology.

"Big Bang" or Gradualism

The pace of development has become a leading question during recent years, with terminology harking back to the creation of the universe.[3] One view holds that the technological transformation should be

---

[3] There are two opposing versions about the origins of the universe. One view, which was derisively dubbed "big bang" by its opponents, holds that the universe began in a fiery cataclysm about 10 billion years ago and might end in an equally spectacular crash billions of years in the future—a religious belief of Hindus and Buddhists. The other view was that the universe had neither a beginning nor an end and that it was infinite and was forever the same. This school of thought known as the "steady state" holds that as the galaxies spread out, new matter would come into existence in the empty space left behind and coagulate to form new galaxies. It should also be noted that according to the big bang school, the early universe, apart from being squeezed together and dense, was also very hot—reaching temperatures of billions of degrees.

very quick, while the other view holds that institutional development is inherently slow. The former school contends that the need for quick results is imperative and inherent in the situation and that tardiness in implementation could be inimical to progress. Thus, results should be obtained before opposition to progress is consolidated. This argument ignores the administrative rationality of policymakers. The question may rise as to whether a policymaker would choose "to make haste slowly" when all indications suggest that quicker results can be procured. In any event, the terms are relative in nature, and the time element in both development scenarios remains to be defined. Moreover, the magnitude of the undertaking will dictate how quickly results are achieved.

For example, standardizing accounting systems could take up to a decade. Some agencies in the United States have pursued standardization for over a decade, and the process is far from complete,[4] partly because the standards themselves have changed during this period in response to conceptual and technological advances. The experience of Australia and New Zealand, which embarked on a major transformation of their financial management systems in the early and mid-1980s, also shows that institutional development is not feasible in a very short period. Clearly, while making efforts to strengthen their systems, governments should also devote their attention to sustaining their efforts over the medium term.

Although accounting reform has not been tainted by politics thus far, the lack of results in the short term could lead to laxity or even abandonment by successor governments. Commitments made in previous years, which appeared binding and inevitable when they were made, suddenly become luxuries that can no longer be afforded. The issue for governments then is how to generate a consensual approach on institutional development that requires more time.

External Assistance or Internal Resources

Developing countries that have begun to reform their accounting systems have an additional choice to make. Existing systems are mostly legacies from the colonial past, and the push for reform, while substantially augmented by domestic inadequacies, stems partly from modernization efforts that originated in the industrial countries. By carefully observing the experiences of the industrial countries, the developing countries can

---

[4]For a case study of the U.S. Department of the Interior, see Kendig (1994). See also New Zealand (1994b).

reap the benefits without repeating the whole evolutionary process. Their gains are the gains of the latecomer. To some extent, the efforts of developing countries to strengthen their accounting systems were spurred by the international organizations, whose efforts over the years have clarified issues, facilitated the transfer of technical knowledge, and improved the acquisition of technical skills. A number of reform programs were also underwritten by international organizations and by donors on a bilateral basis. The issue now confronting policymakers is to determine the relative roles of national authorities and of international agencies.

Over the years, the international agencies have developed their own agenda that is determined in part by their operational interests. This agenda may not be fully congruent with the agenda or the self-recognized needs of the countries. Furthermore, aid from these agencies may not be available on a continuous basis, so that countries that have become dependent on international agencies experience discontinuities. When aid is resumed, it becomes difficult to regain lost momentum. In some cases, the gains may be irretrievably lost and countries may have to begin anew. Also, aid may be in the form of a loan, with an associated impact on the debt-servicing burden of the recipient country.

It is important to recognize that measures aimed at strengthening accounting systems can be formulated and implemented by the reforming country itself. Most countries now have a pool of trained accountants (as distinct from those who acquire skills while working on a job in government) who can help evolve standards and specify the direction of improvements. Acquisition of hardware and associated investment is a separate issue and may involve negotiations for foreign aid. In either event, continuity of financing is essential and must be assured before a country embarks on reform.

Operational Issues

A cursory, cross-country examination of experiences in strengthening accounting systems reveals two types of issues—conceptual and technological. Both these issues offer ample guidance about the details that countries embarking on reform would need to address.

From a conceptual angle, it appears that far more attention has been paid to relationships between government organizations than to the type of internal controls needed in the spending agencies and to the standardization of accounting concepts (as outlined in Chapter 3). This failure to prepare the systems for the application of technology has contributed to a situation in some countries where the individuals who introduced the technology tended to dominate other organizations by carrying out their management and related functions. This administrative "encroachment," or "turf poaching," has created friction among the various parties. The systems became mere instruments for carrying out technical processes in the agencies and for achieving goals and objectives only partially. This problem could have been avoided if there had been a coherent reform plan (even incremental approaches require plans of action) and if a law had been enacted for the purpose. Without a clear and, where appropriate, legal specification of responsibilities, duplication, inconsistencies, and dysfunctional behavior are likely to overwhelm the small gains made otherwise.

Specifically, it is argued that in African countries "information systems fail or underperform more often than they succeed in the public sector in Africa because the saints are few, the demons are many, the wizards are inappropriate, the systems are complex, and the organizations are weak."[5] It is suggested that the authority in public sector operations is personal and procedural and that, in reality these operations are run by fiat rather than by procedure. Hyden (1983) notes, for example, that norms about hiring and firing are rarely observed in Africa, that materials procured for specific purposes are often diverted to other purposes, that attitudes toward planning and scheduling are flexible, that there is long organizational learning, that there is no professionalism in the public service, and that large organizations tend to be divided into smaller ones dominated by individual managers.

Although these characteristics are described as shortcomings common to Africa, a more detailed examination would reveal that they are not always liabilities (indeed, in some ways, they could be considered examples of pioneering leadership and approaches toward managerial flexibility) and are not necessarily limited to Africa. The highly personalized style of administration, which should not be considered a substitute for the rule of law, often proves to be productive in countries where institutions are in their infancy. Observers point out that, in such circumstances, when the leader moves to another position, the reform may suffer discontinuity. Be that as it may, these considerations suggest the continuing need for investment in human resource and organizational development. In the absence of such efforts, investment in technology cannot yield the desired results, and the hope that technology can provide a partial solution to accounting

---

[5]See Peterson (1994, p. 1). The information technology referred to here is largely limited to the application of electronic data-processing technology in the accounting area.

problems would be misplaced. It is clear that administrative systems must be primed for the application of technology.

Other operational issues arise primarily with reference to the application of technology. Although experiences are varied, some common problems emerge. First, far too often the design of systems does not take into account the specific requirements of the agency. For example, in public expenditure management, there are three mutually supporting elements: information architecture (which establishes an overview of the functional processes and related data output structures), systems architecture (comprising a model of the data bases and their flows), and technology architecture (an identification of the needs of each module and determinintion, in that light, of the type of hardware and software appropriate for the purpose). In practice, however, some of these elements may not be fully addressed, and far too frequently, inept designers tend to exploit the situation and view their task as one of promoting whatever hardware and software are available on the market. In the process, the supporting role that technology is expected to play is jeopardized. Second, software may be imposed on the client without proper demonstration of the operational capabilities of the proposed system.[6] This has serious financial and organizational implications, and buyers can only be cautioned about the need for careful appraisal of the software suppliers.[7] Third, countries' procurement policies and procedures may have the effect of acquiring outdated technology primarily because it is less expensive. Such policies have the potential of being very costly in the medium term. Because technology is subject to radical change, it may be more appropriate to choose the more expensive product if it is compatible with the existing system and can meet the agencies' future needs. Finally, the systems may turn out to be far more labor intensive than is supposed at the onset of the reform. The experience of both industrial and

---

[6]Some firms market a product that is now known as "vaporware" and that may be sold to gullible buyers.

[7]The United Nations (1991, pp. 31–38) suggests that governments review the following questions when choosing off-the-shelf software. (1) Can commercial packages truly meet the accounting and volume processing requirements of large government agencies? (2) To what extent would it be appropriate for agencies to customize vendor-supplied core software to cover unmet requirements? (3) Can vendors respond quickly to future needs? (4) Can vendors' software packages meet agencies' management information needs and future direction? (5) Are the time and costs required for implementing off-the-shelf software often understated? (6) Are there long-term risks in relying on vendors to support the software needs of the government? (7) Do the advantages of using commercial packages outweigh the advantages of upgrading the existing agency accounting systems? (8) Can the strategy of using off-the-shelf software be enhanced by developing generic, functional requirements for use throughout the government? (9) How do the use of off-the-shelf software and the government's efforts to standardize data elements relate to each other?

developing countries supports this conclusion. The introduction of technology should not necessarily be resisted. Rather, these issues underline
the need for considerable vigilance and continuous attention to details.

Steps Toward Improvement

In light of the preceding discussion of the issues, a more pragmatic
enumeration of steps toward improvement can be formulated.[8]

(1) Any framework for improvement should start with a review of the
existing systems and the problems associated with them. What are the
systems expected to achieve? How are they performing? To what extent
are problems attributable to outdated processes, inadequate attention to
human resources, and an ill-equipped technological base? What are the
current needs of the users of the system? Because the success of accounting in government depends on the extent to which it is able to anticipate
and meet the needs of policymakers, the review should pay attention to
the changing needs of the users.

(2) In envisaging the answers to these and related issues, policymakers
must recognize two points. First, there may be more than one answer to
each of the questions, and choosing the right one is the crucial part of
the exercise. Second, given the unique nature of government operations,
commercial accounting approaches may need to be extensively adapted
to meet government needs.

(3) The framework developed for overhauling the system should be
applied, initially, on a pilot basis to a few agencies. Such limited application has the potential of containing the risk and revealing problems before they are too entrenched to resolve. Government agencies have
widely differing purposes, missions, and activities, and the experience of
one may not lend itself to replication. Experience remains the best
teacher. More significantly, the pilot applications reveal whether the cost
and benefits are roughly in line with the initial estimates and, if not, what
revisions need to be made.

(4) The experience gained can then be used to formulate laws that will
apply to the whole government. These laws will promote uniform application of the proposed system while fully reflecting government's commitment to the reform. Enactment into law would also provide an
opportunity to harness public opinion in support of the system.

---

[8]The framework largely follows the approach of Lucy Lomax of the U.S. Federal Accounting Standards Board. See Lomax (1994).

Bibliography

Ahmed, Viqar, and Michael Bamberger, *Monitoring and Evaluating Development Projects: The South Asian Experience* (Washington: World Bank, 1989).

American Accounting Association, *Accounting Education and the Third World* (Sarasota, Florida: The Association, 1978).

Apostolou, Nicholas G., and Larry D. Crumbley, *Handbook of Governmental Accounting and Finance* (New York: Wiley, 1988).

Arrow, Kenneth J., *The Economics of Information* (Cambridge, Mass.: Harvard University Press, 1983).

Banca d'Italia, *Ordinary General Meeting of Shareholders* (Abridged Report) (Rome, 1992).

Beauchamp, Chris (1990a), "The Audit of Privatization," *International Journal of Government Auditing*, Vol. 17 (July 1990), p. 9.

———— (1990b), "National Audit Office: Its Role in Privatization," *Public Money and Management*, Vol. 10 (Summer 1990), pp. 55–58.

Berg, Elliot, and United Nations Development Program, *Rethinking Technical Cooperation* (New York: UNDP, 1993).

Berliner, Callie, and James A. Brimson, *Cost Management for Today's Advanced Manufacturing. The CAM-I Conceptual Design* (Boston: Harvard Business School Press, 1988).

Brewer, John, *The Sinews of Power: War, Money and the English State, 1688–1783* (New York: Knopf, 1989).

Brimson, James A., *Activity Accounting: An Activity-Based Costing Approach* (New York: Wiley, 1991).

Broker, Gunther, *Government Securities and Debt Management in the 1990s* (Paris: Organization for Economic Cooperation and Development, 1993).

Canada, Office of the Auditor General, *Annual Report of the Auditor General of Canada for 1993* (Ottawa, 1993).

Chan, James L., ed., *Research in Governmental and Non-Profit Accounting*, Vol. 1 (Greenwich, Conn.: Jai Press, 1985).

Cottarelli, Carlo, *Limiting Central Bank Credit to the Government: Theory and Practice*, IMF Occasional Paper 110 (Washington: IMF, 1993).

Davies, Hywel M., Ali Hashim, and Eduardo Talero, *Information Systems Strategies for Public Financial Management* (Washington: World Bank, 1993).

Durham, Paul, ed., *Output and Performance Measurement in Central Government: Some Practical Achievements* (London: H.M. Treasury, 1987).

Eden, Anthony, *Full Circle: The Memoirs of Anthony Eden* (Boston: Houghton Mifflin, 1960).

Enthoven, Adolf J.H., Jaroslav V. Sokolov, and A.M. Petrachkov, *Doing Business in Russia and the Other Former Soviet Republics* (Montvale, New Jersey: Institute of Management Accountants, 1992).

Ernst & Young, *International Accounting Standards* (Manama, Bahrain, 1993).

European Union, International Monetary Fund, Organization for Economic Cooperation and Development, United Nations, and World Bank, *System of National Accounts 1993* (Brussels/Luxembourg, New York, Paris, Washington, 1993).

Folkerts-Landau, David, Peter Garber, and Timothy D. Lane, "Payment System Reform in Formerly Centrally Planned Countries," in *Building Sound Finance in Emerging Market Economies*, ed. by G. Caprio, D. Folkerts-Landau, and T.D. Lane (Washington: IMF, 1994).

Geiger, Dale R., "Trade Offs Between Comparable Consistency and Relevant Customization in Federal Management Accounting," *The Government Accountants Journal* (Summer 1994), pp. 23–27.

German Foundation for International Development, *Modern Budgeting and Accounting Procedures in Public Finance* (Berlin: The Foundation, 1981).

Goode, Richard, and C. Eugene Steuerle, "Generational Accounts and Fiscal Policy," *Tax Notes*, Vol. 65 (November 1994), pp. 1027–1032.

Gore, Al, *From Red Tape to Results: Creating a Government That Works Better and Costs Less* (New York: Times Books, 1993).

Governmental Accounting Standards Advisory Board, *Objectives of Financial Reporting* (Stamford, Conn.: Financial Accounting Foundation, 1987).

———, *Codification of Governmental Accounting and Financial Reporting Standards* (Norwalk, Conn.: GASB, 1993).

Gupta, M.P., *Government Accounting and Control* (New Delhi: Ashish Publishing House, 1993).

Hardy, Daniel C., and Ashok K. Lahiri, *Cash Shortage in the Former Soviet Union*, IMF Working Paper 94/67 (Washington: IMF, 1994).

Haveman, Robert, "Should Generational Accounts Replace Public Budgets and Deficits?" *Journal of Economic Perspectives*, Vol. 8 (Winter 1994), pp. 95–111.

Herzlinger, Regina E., "Effective Oversight: A Guide for Nonprofit Directors," *Harvard Business Review* (July–Aug. 1994), pp. 52–60.

Hood, Christopher, "A Public Management for All Seasons," *Public Administration*, Vol. 69 (1991).

Hyden, Goran, *No Shortcuts to Progress: African Development Management in Perspective* (Berkeley: University of California Press, 1983).

International Accounting Standards Committee, *International Accounting Standards 1993* (London: The Committee, 1992).

International Capital Markets Group, *Harmonization of International Accounting Standards* (London: ICMG, 1992).

Johnson, H. Thomas, and Robert S. Kaplan, *Relevance Lost: The Rise and Fall of Management Accounting* (Boston, Mass.: Harvard Business School Press, 1987).

Kautilya, *The Arthashastra*, edited, rearranged, translated, and introduced by L.N. Rangarajan (New Delhi: Penguin Books, 1992).

Kendig, William L., "Reinventing Financial Management: Lessons Learned in Standardizing Accounting Systems," *Government Accountants Journal* (Summer 1994), pp. 28–38.

King, M., I. Lapsley, F. Mitchell, and J. Moyes, "Costing Needs and Practices in a Changing Environment. The Potential for ABC in the NHS," *Financial Accountability and Management*, Vol. 10 (May 1994), pp. 143–59.

Kotlikoff, Laurence, J., *Generational Accounting: Knowing Who Pays and When, for What We Spend* (New York: Free Press, 1992).

Leone, Alfredo, "Effectiveness and Implications of Limits on Central Bank Credit to the Government," in *The Evolving Role of Central Banks*, ed. by P. Downes and R. Vaez-Zadeh (Washington: IMF, 1991), pp. 363–413.

Likierman, Andrew, *Public Expenditure: The Public Spending Process* (London: Penguin Books, 1988).

———, "Financial Reporting in the Public Sector," in *Public Sector Accounting and Financial Control*, ed. by D. Henley, C. Holtham, A. Likierman, and J. Perrin (London: Van Nostrand Reinhold International, 3d ed., 1989).

———, "Management Accounting in U.K. Central Government—Some Research Issues," *Financial Accountability and Management*, Vol. 10 (May 1994), pp. 93–115.

Lomax, Lucy, *Approaches to Standardizing Accounting Practices for Improved Financial Management and Decision-Making in U.S. Federal Agencies and Government Ministries in Other Countries* (unpublished; Washington, 1994).

McCulloch, Brian W., "Accounting and Management Reform in New Zealand" (unpublished; Wellington: The Treasury, 1992).

Mikesell, R.M., and Leon E. Hay, *Governmental Accounting* (Homewood, Ill.: Richard D. Irwin, 4th ed., 1969).

New Zealand, The Treasury, *Financial Statements of the Government of New Zealand for the period ended 30 June 1993* (Wellington, 1993).

——— (1994a), *Financial Statements of the Government of New Zealand for the six months ended 31 December 1993* (Wellington, 1994).

——— (1994b), *A Guide to the 1994 Budget Documentation* (Wellington, 1994).

Organization for Economic Cooperation and Development, *The Control and Management of Public Expenditure* (Paris: OECD, 1987).

———, *Measuring Performance and Allocating Resources* (Paris: OECD, 1989).

———, *Accounting for What?: The Value of Accrual Accounting to the Public Sector* (Paris: OECD, 1993).

———, *Public Management Developments: Survey* (Paris: OECD, various issues).

Pendlebury, Maurice, Rowan Jones, and Yusuf Karbhari, "Developments in the Accountability and Financial Reporting Practices of Executive Agencies," *Financial Accountability and Management*, Vol. 10 (Feb. 1994), pp. 33–46.

Pendlebury, Maurice W., ed., *Management Accounting in the Public Sector* (Oxford: Heinemann, 1989).

Peterson, Stephen B., *Saints, Demons, Wizards, and Systems: Why Information Technology Reforms Fail or Underperform in Public Bureaucracies in Africa*, Development Discussion Paper No. 486 (Cambridge, Mass.: Harvard Institute for International Development, 1994).

Pingitzer, Jürgen C., and Bruce J. Summers, "Small Value Transfer Systems," in *The Payment System: Design, Management, and Supervision*, ed. by B. Summers (Washington: IMF, 1994).

Premchand, A., *Performance Budgeting* (Bombay: Academic Books, 1969).

———, *Government Budgeting and Expenditure Controls* (Washington: IMF, 1983).

———, *Public Expenditure Management* (Washington: IMF, 1993).

———, *Changing Patterns in Public Expenditure Management* (unpublished; Washington: IMF, 1994).

———, ed., *Government Financial Management* (Washington: IMF, 1990).

Summers, Bruce J., "Clearing and Payment Systems: The Role of the Central Bank," *Federal Reserve Bulletin*, Vol. 77 (February 1991), pp. 81–91.

———, "The Russian Payment System," in *Building Sound Finance in Emerging Market Economies*, ed. by G. Caprio, D. Folkerts-Landau, and T.D. Lane (Washington: IMF, 1994).

United Kingdom (1994a), *Better Accounting for the Taxpayer's Money: Resource Accounting and Budgeting in Government* (London: HMSO, 1994).

——— (1994b), *Fundamental Review of Running Costs* (London: H.M. Treasury, 1994).

———, Department of Health and Office of Population Censuses and Surveys (1994c), *The Government's Expenditure Plans 1994–95 to 1996–97: Departmental Report* (London: HMSO, 1994).

United Nations, *A Manual for Programme and Performance Budgeting* (New York: 1965).

———, *Government Accounting and Financial Reporting in Developing Countries*, TCD/SEM.87/3, INT/86/R58 (New York, 1988).

———, *Computerization of Government Accounting in Developing Countries*, TCD/SEM.91/2, INT/90/R79 (New York, 1991).

———, Conference on Trade and Development, *Accounting, Valuation, and Privatization* (New York, 1993).

United Nations, Economic and Social Commission for Asia and the Pacific, *The Control and Management of Public Expenditure: Issues and Experience in Asian Countries* (Bangkok, 1993).

United States, Congressional Budget Office, *Using Performance Measures in the Federal Budget Process* (Washington, 1993).

United States, Federal Accounting Standards Advisory Board, *Financial Resources, Funded Liabilities, and Net Financial Resources of Federal Entities* (Exposure Draft) (Washington, 1991).

———, *Accounting for Selected Assets and Liabilities* (Washington, 1992).

——— (1993a), *Accounting for Direct Loans and Loan Guarantees* (Washington, 1993).

——— (1993b), *Accounting for Inventory and Related Property* (Washington, 1993).

——— (1993c), *Objectives of Federal Financial Reporting* (Washington, 1993).

——— (1994a), *Accounting for Liabilities of the Federal Government* (Exposure Draft) (Washington, 1994).

——— (1994b), *Entity and Display* (Exposure Draft) (Washington, 1994).

——— (1994c), *Managerial Cost Accounting Standards for the Federal Government* (Exposure Draft) (Washington, 1994).

United States, General Accounting Office, *Title 2, Accounting, GAO Policy and Procedures Manual for Guidance of Federal Agencies* (Washington, 1988).

———, *Employee Benefits: Companies' Retiree Health Liabilities Large, Advance Funding Costly* (Washington, 1989).

——— (1990a), *Cost Accounting Issues: Survey of Cost Accounting Practices at Selected Agencies* (Washington, 1990).

——— (1990b), *Hazardous Waste: Funding of Postclosure Liabilities Remains Uncertain* (Washington, 1990).

———— (1990c), *Public Debt: Management Actions Needed to Ensure More Accurate Accounting* (Washington, 1990).

————, *Financial Audit: FSLIC Resolution Fund's 1989 Financial Statements* (Washington, 1991).

———— (1992a), *Navy Ships: Plans and Anticipated Liabilities to Terminate SSN-21 Program Contracts* (Washington, 1992).

———— (1992b), *Pension Plans: Hidden Liabilities Increase Claims Against Insurance Program* (Washington, 1992).

————, *Environmental Liability: Property and Casualty Insurer Disclosure of Environmental Liabilities* (Washington, 1993).

————, and Canada, Office of the Auditor General, *Federal Government Reporting Study: A Joint Study* (Gaithersburg, MD: USGAO, 1986).

United States, General Accounting Office, Joint Financial Management Improvement Program, *Financial Handbook for Federal Executives and Managers* (Washington, 1991).

———— (1992a), *Facing the Facts of the CFO Act* (Washington, 1992).

———— (1992b), *Strategies to Improve Communication between Program and Financial Managers* (Washington, 1992).

———— (1994a), *Reinventing Government, The Financial Manager's Role* (Washington, 1994).

———— (1994b), *Report on Financial Management Improvements 1993* (Washington, 1994).

United States, Office of Management and Budget, "Form and Content of Agency Financial Statements," OMB Bulletin No. 93–02 (Washington, 1992).

————, *Federal Financial Management Status Report and 5-Year Plan* (Washington, 1993).

————, *Budget of the United States Government: Analytical Perspectives, Fiscal Year 1995* (Washington, 1994).

United States, Treasury Department, Financial Management Service (1989a), *FMS Disbursement Guide* (Washington, 1989).

———— (1989b), *Now That You're a Certifying Officer* (Washington: 1989).

————, *Vendor Express and the Vendor (Customer)* (Washington, 1990).

World Bank (1994a), *Adjustment in Africa: Reforms, Results and the Road Ahead* (New York: Oxford University Press, 1994).

———— (1994b), *Averting the Old-Age Crisis* (Oxford, England; New York: Published for the World Bank by Oxford University Press, 1994).

———— (1994c), *Governance: The World Bank's Experience* (Washington, 1994).